Dog Training and Eight Faces of Aggressive Behavior

Dog Training and Eight Faces of Aggressive Behavior

A Master's Solution to Barkers, Growlers and Biters

Matthew Duffy

Copyright © 2013 Matthew Duffy
All rights reserved.
ISBN: 1492336718
ISBN 13: 9781492336716

Dedication

To my father, Paul Edward Duffy,
the man who taught me about devotion:
to God,
to family,
to duty.

Contents

Dedication v
Biography ix
Recognition..xi
Introduction...xiii
Chapter One: Understanding Canine Aggression and Its Management 1
Chapter Two: Primary Handlers, Learning and Rules 15
Chapter Three: Dog against Dog Aggression 37
Chapter Four: Predatory Aggression 57
Chapter Five: Defensive Aggression 79
Chapter Six: Territorial Aggression 101
Chapter Seven: Protest Aggression 121
Chapter Eight: Intolerance Aggression 143
Chapter Nine: Possessive Aggression 161
Chapter Ten: Social Aggression... 187
Conclusion 213

Biography

Matthew Duffy was born and raised in southern Indiana, the beautiful hilly country overlooking the mighty Ohio River. His natural rapport with animals became apparent at the young age of thirteen when Matthew worked as a mounted trail guide for a local riding stable. After years of working with horses, Matthew turned his full attention to dogs. He completed a comprehensive professional dog trainer's course in 1980 and soon became the head trainer at a prominent kennel in Louisville, Kentucky. In 1983, Matthew entered into a partnership with a dog training center in Indiana and several years later established his own training facility, Advanced Training Kennel, Inc.

During his formal study of behavior at Indiana University Southeast, Matthew was inducted into the National Honor Society in Psychology. Through his study and early experiences working with the Floyd County Police Department as a K9 handler, titling dogs and belonging to the United Schutzhund Clubs of America, and attending numerous working-dog seminars that Matthew was able to develop his unique approach to dog training by way of canine self-control.

Currently, Matthew owns and operates Duffy's Dog Training Center LLC, where he oversees the instruction of several hundred dogs and their owners annually. A master of his trade, Matthew Duffy has trained literally thousands of dogs over the past three decades for every imaginable purpose: family obedience, handicap assistance, search and rescue, police work along with illicit drug detection, AKC competition and Schutzhund sport.

Over the last decade Matthew has trained dogs in termite sent detection and bed bug sent detection. Since 2008 Matthew has been conducting Quarterly Pet Safety Seminars for Norton/ Suburban Hospital system in Louisville Kentucky. Matthew has published a training book, <u>Ten Natural Steps to Training the Family Dog</u> *Building a Positive Relationship* and DVDs, <u>Ten Natural Steps to Training the Family Dog</u>, *Building a Positive Relationship* I and II. In 2009 Matthew was invited to be a guest instructor for the Annual K9 Street Survival Seminar in the Smokies for police K-9 units and has instructed every year since. Recently, Matthew was invited to assist with preparing Naval Special Warfare dog teams to deploy for active assignments.

Matthew's latest endeavor was establishing Whitefangventures.com, a ground breaking interactive dog training website. The goal of WhiteFangVentures.com is to make a dog trainer's lifetime of information readily accessible in a format that can reach out to all those who may benefit.

Even now, any working day of the week you'll find Matthew with a leash in his hand.

Recognition

Editors, formatters, sounding boards and photographers are the behind-the-scenes cavalry for every writer. For a small time, self-published, author like me those roles are filled by only a few. A few courageous friends, along with my son and daughter, made up the entire editorial staff for this book. They volunteered for those tedious editing and formatting tasks partly because they believe in the usefulness of this practical dog handling guide. Cathy, John, Zachary, Heidi and Alex assisted me mostly because I asked them to. Being of the highest caliber people, they jumped into the project with resolve and enthusiasm.

Thank you Dr. John Parker for applying your scientific mind, once more, to such meticulous editing; I can think of no one else as capable or willing to work so hard in the name of friendship. Your mental acuity has helped immeasurably to transform a raw manuscript into a finished work. I am most appreciative for your company and friendship over the years.

Thank you Zachary Duffy for tackling the job no one wants; the formatting, embedding and overall conforming to printing demands. You are an interface extraordinaire and there would be no book for anyone to read without your considerable effort. I am fortunate to have had the opportunity to work with my son on such a personally important project.

Thank you Heidi O'Bryant for the final once over; your discerning eyes apply the necessary polish to bring about a finished work. It's been a genuine pleasure to collaborate with my intelligent and hardworking daughter during this undertaking. I give you the honor of the final read for as long as you are willing.

Thank you my dearest Cathy Cantu. In all my years of professional instruction, I've not come across your equal in terms of zest and hunger for dog training truths. Your indefatigable pursuit of canine behavior knowledge has inspired me for nearly a decade. I can't imagine writing about dogs without my best friend to consult with. You make me feel much more important than I actually am. What a gift it has been to be able to share this portion of my life with you.

Many thanks to the training center clan: Dave Benson, Katherine Bosley, Josh Decker, Tyler Oldmann and Heidi O'Bryant. The countless hours we have spent training and discussing behavior together have quickly turned into years. Much of the material for this book has come about as the fruit of our combined labor. I will always be indebted for your comradery and efforts that have gone above and beyond the call of duty.

Thanks my friend, Alex Krljas. Your skill with a camera and professional direction made all of our photo sessions not only productive, but enjoyable. How nice it was having a dog man behind the camera helping me capture canine behavior.

Introduction

Can the subject of family dog hostility be dealt with adequately in a book? This is a nagging question that's lingered with me for years. After an active, full career in the dog training industry, this book represents my best attempt to effectively address the topic. In regards to study and hands on experience, not many people could have devoted more time and energy towards this subject than I have. Even so, I've been reluctant to tackle this project because of the emotional nature of the issue. The owner of an aggressive dog is usually stressed over the potentially injurious behavior their treasured pet displays. Embarrassment about the disagreeable conduct and frustration over how to handle it, compound this underlying anxiety. On the flip side of this coin, are the individuals receiving the family pet's hostility who usually experience fear or react with anger when exposed to such intense confrontations. From a professional trainer's standpoint, my services are sought out because the dog owners really care about the welfare of their pet and those who will be exposed to him. Understandably, the owners don't want to see their canine companion or innocent beings uncomfortable and distressed during the behavior shaping process. However, the very act of trying to ward off an assertive canine, or quash the emotional explosion of a fearfully defensive dog, is distressing for all concerned. It appears from all angles that dealing with unwanted aggression in the family dog is an emotional business. My calm presence and confident reassurance during in-person instruction is a strong mitigating force that helps ensure a positive out-come for these, often emotional, training experiences. I hope the words in the following chapters will give you a similar sense of a balanced presence.

For dog training purposes, hostile canine behavior is best viewed as an emotional fire. Viscerally reacting to a dog's aggressive conduct with an equally emotional response, whether fearful or angry, is only going to fuel a fire that is already burning out of control. The most productive way for a handler to respond to his dog's inappropriate assertive behavior is with calm and decisive action. Effectively controlling the explosive situation without getting caught up in the emotion is a tall order for new handlers but that is what this book will help you achieve. Keep in mind that calm and firm are not mutually exclusive. The greatest service I can give to my clients is the demonstration of this maxim while handling their dogs.

Unlike my obedience guide, "Ten Natural Steps to Training the Family Dog", this book is less like a step-by-step "How-to" manual and much more of a template for establishing relationship parameters. Effective aggression control training is a process sensitive to a canine student's emotional state and personality characteristics. Even though temperament and disposition should be taken into account with any kind of structured dog training, successful hostility management hinges on it. With basic obedience instruction, training protocol can be generalized and remain quite effective across a wide spectrum of canine personalities. To successfully manage an aggressive dog however, a handler needs to tailor the training approach to closely fit the student's inherent drives and aversions.

The scholastic study of animal behavior is a terrific foundation for understanding dog training methodology. However, the application of behavior shaping techniques can be a very tricky business because of the multitude of variables. Nowhere is this truer than in dealing with canine aggression. The strength of a dog's personality, energy level, past experiences, and the intensity of distractions all greatly affect a dog's response to his environment as well as his handler. It stands to reason that with all the possible combinations and variables, there is someone reading this book that owns a dog, lives in a uniquely complex environment, or possesses the personality that makes training success nearly impossible, but I assure you that unusual situations like this represent a small minority.

I've been afforded many thousands of opportunities to both enhance and curb the aggressive potential in dogs. With hunting, security, schutzhund sport, and police canines my job is to build strong, (channeled) assertive responses. On the polar opposite side of the dog world, my services are rendered to quash hostile conduct as with most of the aggressive family pets I meet. It

Introduction

became apparent to me after years of working with both ends of this behavioral spectrum that the best way to manage hostile behavior was through the self control that canine manners and distraction conditioning create. So, I began teaching assertive dogs how to control their drive, energy as well as emotion, by using incentives and deterrents (rather than formal commands) under the challenge of distractions. Hands free control over the potentially hostile dog came before the introduction or the use of formal directives. This approach applied to and worked equally well with either working canines, or the family pet.

The "hold and bark" exercise at Schutzhund competition

I decided, in this guide, that detailed real life examples would be the best means to illustrate the range of handling techniques I use to control hostility. Every human-dog relationship is unique and nowhere in the canine training world is that more apparent than in directing the behavior of an assertive dog. Use the instruction examples I give you as a guide to structuring your own training plan. If safety is compromised during the execution of your plan, or your dog's hostility steadily worsens then stop training immediately and seek out qualified (check resumes and references for the appropriate experience) professional help.

It will quickly become apparent as you read through this manual that the Five Handling Manners of my basic obedience program constitute the foundation for managing all eight faces of dog aggression. Composure, Food Control, Visitor Control, Open Door Control, and the Walking exercise represent the necessary requisites that every assertive canine must possess before any specific or complex behavior shaping begins. These canine self control exercises represent the starting point even when I conduct workshops or seminars for professional handlers and their high intensity dogs. I consider the five handling manners pivotal when directing the drives of aggressive police and military dogs. These primary obedience exercises work progressively, one on top of the other, to galvanize three canine responsibilities that are of paramount importance to any dog training program.

1. The canine student is responsible for containing his drive and energy.
2. The canine student should defer to his handler before committing to serious action.
3. The canine student should remain mindful of his handler's policies while in proximity of distractions.

Introduction

A police dog putting natural aggression to use

Once a dog embraces these self control duties, he will be mentally free to focus on the designated skills of higher training. Think of complete dog training as the combination of two distinct pursuits: the development of casual canine self-control, and the building of formal command responses. Hostility management is the process of curbing and channeling intense energy, so plan on using all the tools in your dog trainer's box to harness this explosive potential. Support your dog's energy channeling efforts and his formal command training with a foundation of canine manners. This will ensure a healthful progression in his behavior shaping instruction.

Chapter One

Understanding Canine Aggression and Its Management

Casual but absolute control without the use of harsh or emotional communication from the handler, that's the approach I'd longed for in the early days of my career, only there was no one around to demonstrate how that could be done. Truthfully, I don't think anyone thought about this kind of self control training as a technique or as a means to an end like I do. In my first book (Ten Natural Steps to Training the Family Dog) I laid out the principles of this self control training technique at the very beginning, in the handling manners section, even though this book only deals with basic obedience issues. The reason I begin basic obedience training with this self control technique is the same reason I employ it to control aggression. It is the single best way I have found, in all these years, to get a dog to think clearly. If a dog thinks clearly his lessons are truly learned, and he will efficiently assimilate the necessary information. In regards to hostile canines, efficient assimilation of intended information corresponds to less rule testing and a higher degree of safety.

Aggression is a powerful tool! When a dog figures that out, he's typically not going to relinquish that power willingly, and when you finally get him to acquiesce, he's definitely not going to forget about the mighty sword he once wielded. Many dog owners and some professionals in the canine industry don't seem to recognize (or won't accept) that the lion's share of assertive dogs get a rush out of a hostile display, or at the very least, appreciate this behavior's effect. The usual adjectives that accompany an aggressive dog into our training center are: poor, pitiful, abused, and scared. Often what I see walking through the door on four feet is: cocky, assertive, dominant, and combative. Don't get me wrong, we do get our share of truly pitiful cases; dogs who suffer because they were robbed of handling and socializing while they developed or dogs who have been left to fend for themselves in household packs that operate more like a "Lord of the Flies" society than a family. These cases, I assure you, represent only a small percentage of the hostile canines we handle year in and year out.

Recognition of this emotional rush, and the value some dogs place on assertive behavior, helps a handler understand why it's such a challenge to quash. When we discourage a dog from displaying hostility, we're essentially telling him to put that effective tool back in the box. We are robbing him of a familiar emotional high. Put in these terms, one can appreciate the great effort required to facilitate meaningful behavioral change in an aggressive dog. I would like to humanize things for just a moment to bring our behavior shaping task into proper perspective. Most of us, at some period in our lives, have had to deal with a hot tempered human being. Maybe like me, you were the person others dreaded to be around when emotional control was lost. Despite all the tools I was born with as an intelligent human being, and all the good behavioral skills I had acquired through life experiences and study, I was only able to bring my temper under control with wheel barrows of effort and concentration over years of practice. I can attest to the exhilaration that accompanies an uninhibited tantrum and I've witnessed others giving way to my temper, similar to how a dog could perceive the same situation. So viscerally, selfishly speaking, stimulating things can be associated with hostile displays. Of course we all know that truly good things don't come about from loss of emotional control, it just feels that way to the aggressor (at least for a moment).

Anthropomorphizing is risky business when it comes to dog training because it often leads to incorrect interpretations and erroneous conclusions. However, I think this particular analogy is helpful to understand the effort required by a dog to control his hostile expressions. I have also noticed a significant increase in handling diligence with clients after discussing my insights about the similarities between human tantrums and dog aggression.

There is no doubt in my mind that the ability I have to understand, empathize, and train aggressive dogs has been enhanced by my own personal battle with an Irish temper!

The triggers for my labile temper didn't always seem to be predictable although there were some guaranteed conditions that would always elicit an intense response. I believe my inability to foresee and prepare for impending triggers, made the challenge of controlling my temper much greater. With little warning, I was easily caught off guard and completely consumed by a dark mood. I was able to identify most of the triggers or conditions for my temper flare ups, and this allowed me the time I needed to divert my energy and emotions to neutral ground before being totally consumed by the negative situation. **Identifying the potential triggers and redirecting the dog's mind before being lost in the throes of rage, is also the key to success when working with hostile canine personalities.**

A convenient aspect of working with dogs, being the limbic animals that they are, is the simplistic nature of their aggressive triggers. Few would disagree with the statement that dogs are emotional animals, but their emotional composition is not nearly as complex as ours. So, identifying and avoiding the stimuli for hostile responses is a much easier task than it is for the humans. This idea directly relates to the title of this book, Eight Faces of Aggressive Behavior. The faces I refer to in the title are actually the categories of common hostility triggers that I have identified over the years. The identification of these stimuli and the descriptions of the possible responses from an aggressive dog exposed to these triggers are not the result of a scientific study. These faces represent common knowledge and my personal observations carefully outlined for the purpose of effective training and instruction. Being able to identify and discuss the parameters of a hostile situation involving a dog allows the trainer to set up similar situations with a plan to bring about improved results. The ability to categorize and describe the specifics of a dog's aggressive behavior makes it much easier for the owner to understand what is really taking place during the experience. Removing the ambiguity of why the dog responded a certain way in a particular situation almost immediately removes the fear and frustration many owners experience when handling their hostile companion. The specific knowledge of why and when aggression occurs lends itself directly to precaution, not worry, and precaution leads directly to safety which is the primary purpose for this book.

A military, Special Forces dog ready for a patrol exercise

I think it's best to think of an aggressive dog as being hard wired that way, in other words, predisposed to respond with emotional force to certain stimuli in particular situations. Any potentially hostile canine, wild or domestic, was born with his aggressive tools already in his box. In wild situations these tools will be the difference between who gets to eat and who doesn't, who gets to breed and who doesn't, and who has control over territory and who doesn't. So from a survival standpoint, those who have the best tools and learn how to use them pass on their genes; that is the name of the game for all creatures. **Viewing assertiveness in your canine companion as a tool that needs to be controlled rather than a shameful demonic spirit that needs to be exorcised will make all the difference in the way you approach training.**

Keep in mind, with any kind of dog training the handler's attitude is everything. As the handler, you are the captain of the team and the captain establishes the tempo for his four legged team mate. Trying to manage your dog's hostile behavior with anger or hysteria is simply dumping emotional fuel on an already blazing emotional fire. By placating or consoling your aggressive companion, you are only empowering him. The handling approach I will teach you in these pages centers around confidence in understanding what kind of canine behavior you're dealing with, and stressing calmness in knowing that it's a natural part of a canine's personality. Regardless of what type of hostility your dog expresses, our goal in training will be realistic. We can't eliminate this hostile potential, but we can restrain it with rules and channel it with our own guidelines. Remember, dogs are born with these tools, and not all canine aggression is unwanted. For instance, if you owned a working sheep or cattle ranch, an assertive livestock dog would be an invaluable teammate when managing the daily chores. Often times a police officer's best back up is his canine partner with highly developed aggressive skills. Moving closer to home, an effective watchdog is a working animal with his hostile potential channeled by the owner's guidelines (hopefully). This same idea of directing and developing a dog's assertive potential applies equally well to hunting dogs. For literally thousands of years mankind has selectively bred Canis familiaris to suit his wants and needs, and one of the traits that humans valued and chose to enhance or pass on was aggression. Whether for the purpose of guardian, hunter, herder or war dog, we wanted a companion with moxie! So realistically speaking, humans helped design the blueprint for the mental and emotional circuitry of our contemporary canine companion.

A mix of hounds and their handlers after successfully bagging a bear

Hostile potential in a dog is neither good nor bad; it simply is or is not present to a degree where it needs to be curbed. The chapters in this book are set up to help you identify what type of aggressive expression your dog may exhibit. By identifying the particular switch or triggers that set your dog into hostile action, we will label the type of unwanted behavior that needs to be addressed. For example, in chapter three we tackle dog on dog hostility, which means a canine targets other canines (usually dogs outside the family pack) as threatening competition, and he reacts aggressively. In chapter eight I'll take you through the ins and outs of intolerance aggression, which is deals with inappropriate boundaries the four legged student has set up inside his household, having little to do with a specific target.

As you can see with these two brief descriptions, the stimulus for canine aggression can be target based or situational. The direction of training is directly linked to the type of hostility needing to be quashed, that's why it is so critical to accurately assess the cause and effect in each case. The eight categories of canine aggression I describe in this book are only guidelines for handlers to operate by, and by no means represent the exact parameters in which an assertive pet is bound. Often we witness blends of these categories like the case of a defensive dog (a canine that is uncomfortable around strangers) who lacks the confidence or courage to patrol a large territory, but who can be quite formidable in guarding a small area such as a vehicle or pen. Many dogs are quite accomplished at wielding their aggressive sword under varied conditions such as possessiveness over treasures, assertive resistance to a handler's command, and bullying passive members of the family. The subdivisions of aggressive behavior outlined in each chapter are simply descriptive tools I've found to be very useful in both dog training and handler instruction. As a trainer, I need to establish a behavior shaping plan that addresses the specific issues of the dog in training or I won't be successful; these categories give me the direction I need. As an owner, you need to know why your dog reacts the way he does in certain situations, or to certain stimuli, so that you will have the confidence to follow training protocol.

For the owner, successful management of unwanted canine behavior should be thought of as the sum of three parts:
1. Accurate assessment of the problem.
2. Development of the appropriate training plan.
3. Diligent handler follow-through.

In the following chapters I will help you evaluate your dog effectively, I will help you establish a directed training protocol, and I will motivate you to follow through with the plan to ensure success! My job is to give you the confidence to be a team leader. Ultimately that is what all dogs are really looking for a leader, a captain, an alpha. If you don't fill that role your dog might, and that is a guaranteed recipe for disaster. Follow the rules I lay out in this book and there will be no disaster, just harmony.

For the dog, successful management of unwanted behavior boils down to three responsibilities:
1. Energy and drive control.
2. Deferring to the handler.
3. Mindfulness around distractions.

Within each chapter dealing with a particular form of hostile expression, I will explain how to utilize command free manners, or self control exercises, to curb your dog's aggression. Changing a dog's automatic response to a stimulus is the only way to ensure self-restraint in a potentially hostile situation. Over time, we gradually eliminate the need for handler intervention through association. We're going to give our canine in training the freedom to choose his course of action in any given situation. **Our job as handlers is to supply the appropriate consequence in connection with the dog's chosen course of action**. That is, if my canine companion decides to growl at Uncle Charlie for walking past the feeding dish, I'm going to give my assertively possessive dog a sharp leash and collar correction. However, if my four legged friend peacefully (albeit reluctantly) moves out of Charlie's way as he passes by the feeding dish, I will walk to his side and offer some genuine praise. **Even though it may mean having a cumbersome training environment, take the necessary steps (utilizing secure training collars, longer leashes and barriers) to ensure safety for all concerned well before any interaction is allowed or before any handling begins.**

What I've just described is the heuristic learning process (trial and error), one of the primary modes of information gathering that all canines (wild and domestic) utilize. A handler must carefully monitor these learning situations to ensure his dog walks away from the experience with the desired lesson learned. Imagine Uncle Charlie backing away from the growling dog and the feeding dish, and let's say although I halfheartedly step in with a verbal reprimand (of little consequence to most dogs), Charlie decides to avoid any future conflict by retreating back into the living room. What the dog is going to learn from this experience is that people back down from his growl. The dog is quite capable of guarding his own feeding dish, and although the captain of the team was a little upset, nothing much negative came out of the whole growling incident. The dog in this scenario will quickly sum up what's just been learned as, more good than bad comes from guarding the feeding dish, so why give up the growling that seems to come so naturally anyway?

Directing a young police dogs combativeness

Now let's adjust the learning situation a little bit, rather than casually stepping in with a reprimand for my house pet's inappropriate behavior, I will decisively administer a leash and collar correction that immediately grabs my dog's full attention. Once I have redirected my student's attention from the importance of the dish to the importance of the team captain, I will implore Uncle Charlie to finish his route past the feeding station to his original destination. With these two simple changes in the learning experience we're able to convince our dog that no good comes from growling at Charlie. Because no one backed down except our overly zealous guard dog, the feeding dish was left at Charlie's disposal and the captain of the team has no qualms about delivering impressive, negative consequences.

During a successful training scenario, in addition to experiencing the negative effects of growling, a dog needs to be immediately exposed to the aggression trigger so the exercise may be repeated with a new, pleasant outcome. Now let's suppose Uncle Charlie walks by the feeding dish and instead of our canine student growling, this time the dog musters the self control to turn his head and let the visitor pass by his precious dish. In return for his Herculean effort, the dog in training should receive lavish praise (maybe even a treat as a bonus) absent of lingering emotion associated to the disappointment from the first episode. With this straightforward training process, a dog can clearly connect his negative action (as the handler views it) to the handler's corrective (non-emotional) reaction, or likewise he will connect his positive behavior to a genuinely positive consequence. A handler must also accept the fact that his trusted canine companion may never like his dear uncle, at least not too close to the feeding station, but tolerance and/or harmony is the goal. The canine student will work toward this goal out of respect for his team leader and the consequences that the leader may deliver.

Besides trial and error, modeling is another learning system our dogs depend on when gathering information. As far as your pet is concerned there is no one more important to model after than the leader of the pack (that should be you and not another canine family member!). Remember, dogs in all social settings are looking for a leader. Because they are pack animals by design, dogs need social structure for their health and stability. A leader is not simply an option; it's an absolute necessity for harmony in the family. You must establish yourself as the captain of the family team by demonstrating to the canine teammates that you're the policy-setter and a consequence-supplier. You should also exude calmness when interacting with your dog, or dogs. I believe that calmness is one of the most important characteristics of a good handler, because tranquil handling is conducive to clear thinking, and clear thinking is an all important requisite for learning. Through modeling your canine companion always has access to a reaction gauge (you) for any given situation. Keep in mind, the handler sets the tone or the mood for the living environment. It doesn't matter if you're dealing with Uncle Charlie and the feeding dish or guests at the front door; take the appropriate action while conveying that everything is going to be OK!

In this guide to aggressive behavior management you will find that I avoid using formal commands to initially control a hostile canine. Instead, I choose to control the situation with properly administered consequences. Here is why, allowing for the time it takes a handler to deliver a command, plus the time it takes a dog to process the information and respond (or not) then add the time it takes for the handler to dole out the appropriate consequence in connection to the dog's response results in too many steps, over too much time, to build the desired automatic response pattern. Besides, with a formal command approach to hostility control, the handler will always need to be quick on the draw with the directives in order to quash unwanted aggression. My preferred plan for controlling unwanted hostile behavior is to establish a simple association between aggressive display and an effective negative consequence. With this instantaneous action- reaction approach, a dog will quickly develop a new and better response to the aggression trigger that will become automatic, thereby gradually eliminating the handler's role in this kind of situation. I want to be clear, formal commands are indispensable in a complete dog training program. They are needed for direction and the elicitation of specific responses only after the dog demonstrates adequate self control around his aggression triggers.

There are the five core concepts the self control technique revolves around:
1. A dog's freedom to choose.
2. Timely consequences.
3. A calm handler.
4. Proper use of distractions.
5. Safe confinement for unsupervised canine students.

Assuming our domestic dogs (like their wild counterparts) are smarter than turtles, the freedom to choose a course of action allows them to learn through the natural heuristic process of trial and error. The success or failure of their preferred course is defined by the timely consequence the handler attaches to it. For example, commitment to inappropriate behavior yields a negative consequence such as training collar action, and commitment to desirable behavior brings about the positive consequences of physical caress, verbal praise or food reward. A calm handler is of key importance for several reasons. First and foremost, the handler being the captain of the human-animal team sets the example for the team's reaction to the multifarious aspects of the ambient environment. Dogs learn from modeling much like humans do and team members often look to the captain for the appropriate response. By promoting calmness the handler is setting the stage for clear thinking because a hysterical, panicky or enraged mindset is not conducive to information absorption or retention. When a handler demonstrates calmness in the thick of activity, he's demonstrating to the dog, the confidence and control aspects of a leader.

Nearly every activity in this physical world that you and your dog engage in is inundated with distractions. So teaching your dog specific responses to stimuli without the presence of realistic distractions is a colossal waste of time and effort. Choosing the correct intensity, frequency, and proximity of a training distraction can be extremely exacting, but it is so necessary. The optimal moment of entry and exit for a distraction is also a critical consideration when working an aggressive dog around his target of choice. Given the multifarious nature of canine dispositions, coupled with the endless variety of possible distractions, it's no wonder the task of effective training can seem so daunting if hostility is factored in.

Last but definitely not least is the concept of safe confinement, since we count on trial and error as our canine's primary learning system, we better make darn sure that the appropriate consequence is associated with the dog's chosen course of action. This means through the duration of our companion's training, he needs to be supervised at all times by a primary handler when free to act upon his environment or fellow inhabitants. If (and this is a big if) for any reason, as the designated primary handler, you are unable or unwilling (it is ok to be unwilling) for a period of time to supervise your canine student, tuck him away in a proper safe place (i.e. a crate, cage, pen, run or fenced yard). If due diligence is not given to supervision and confinement, your companion may learn that chasing the cat through the house and under the bed while you (the primary handler) were otherwise occupied (taking a shower) was just as invigorating as it was three weeks ago before training began. In this case the lessons learned by the dog would be something like this, the cat is still his to abuse, when the handler is in the shower the new rules don't apply, and being sneaky and clever works to his advantage so sharpen these skills. These are not exactly the lessons the handler had in mind to convey, but these were the lessons learned none the less. So beware, new canine students are analogous to hungry, self serving sponges soaking up all the environmental information they can hold. I admire my German Shepherd's appetite for data, but I also try not to forget I control, in large part, what he's allowed to soak up.

These five core concepts set in motion the development of the three pivotal canine responsibilities (1. Energy and drive control, 2. Deference to the handler, 3. Mindfulness among distractions) which are almost solely capable of controlling unwanted aggression in your dog. Of course, dependable response to formal commands such as: heel, down, stay, and come are a plus, they should not be expected to control aggression on their own. Even though these basic principles of aggression control apply equally well to working dogs (police, hunting, security, competition and herding types), this is not a training manual for the promotion and direction of aggressive drive and energy. There are many special considerations that go along with training canines for this purpose, not to mention the exponential increase in handling effort and finesse required to properly handle a true working animal.

Although empirical in nature, this practical guide for handling assertive dogs was not written by a researcher to be part of a scientific study, nor did the data come from a laboratory. For the most part, the straightforward information in the following pages is delivered to you in layman's terms by a professional dog trainer directly from the working field and home environment. The information gleaned from this work should bring you and your dog, to some degree, a better quality of life. Remember, aggressive dogs weren't born evil; they were simply born more challenging.

Chapter Two

Primary Handlers, Learning and Rules

I still remember the very first dog bite I received. I was about six years old and playing with little, plastic soldiers in the gutter in front of my house when my best friend Freddy came over with some of his soldiers to join me. Taffy, his not so friendly Cocker Spaniel, came with him. I never did like that dog, but I did like Freddy so Taffy was part of the deal. Like many of the American Cockers today, Taffy didn't put up with any nonsense and she was known for biting people who boldly walked up to within spitting distance of her house, (and I do mean HER house). No one in Freddy's family was foolish enough to attempt to take hold of that little, blonde devil as long as she was busy laying down the law with some outsider. On occasion, Freddy's mom or dad would scream out "Taffy, suppertime". If Taffy were hungry enough or simply bored with holding a passerby at bay, she would pull away from her perceived duties of terrorizing the neighborhood and head into the house for some sort of food reward for a job well done. The behavior Taffy was being rewarded for, attacking a neighbor or coming home, was never really clear to anyone including Taffy. As far as I was concerned, I didn't care how they got her in; bribery, fear tactics, or a wild animal net, it didn't matter to me. Just get her off the streets!

I made a habit of taking a "shield" with me when I visited Freddy's house to play, usually my bike; I would call him from the front yard because Taffy didn't like me on her porch. Sometimes Taffy didn't like Freddy on her porch either. Believe it or not, back in my childhood days in my old neighborhood, it wasn't a big deal to have an aggressive Cocker running loose occasionally biting someone. I really liked Freddy and his sisters and my parents liked his parents, so that meant we had to put up with Taffy. Compared to the litigious, avoid responsibility, time we live in now, I grew up in a different world.

On this particular morning, Taffy decided she was going to chew on my prized army tank, so like most six year olds I reacted viscerally and quickly snatched the tank from the devil's jaws. Taffy seemed stunned by my brief display of moxie, because she actually paused for a moment before she punished me for such insolence. And punish she did, delivering a severe bite, to my little kid belly. I still remember being more upset over my bloody torn shirt than I was over my punctured skin. My dad's reaction to my tears and torn shirt was indicative of the times. While he cleaned me up and helped with changing the shirt, I explained what happened. My dad's advice as I headed back outside was to leave the dog alone. Like I said, it was a different world. There were no calls to Freddy's parents, there was no worry over Taffy's vaccination status, and there was no call for any action as far as my dad was concerned. It may seem like he didn't care, but that's not true. In his assessment I was fundamentally sound, and dog bites were simply not a big deal. I'm quite sure if I had suffered from Taffy's attacks more frequently, my parents would have taken a different course of action. They were reasonable people and just shared a common belief that everybody has been bitten by a dog. They believed most of the dogs owned by good people are inoculated against rabies. Besides this shared lackadaisical approach to dog aggression, my parents and I had another reason to be so accepting of dog bites, his name was Kaiser. He was our formidable German Shepherd who had on a few occasions jumped his measly four foot high fence to inflict his own justice on some evildoer.

One evildoer turned out to be, my best friend. Freddy and I used to wrestle all the time, as boys are inclined to do. Since Freddy was a few years older than me, he was considerably bigger and stronger and usually dominated the wrestling match. On one such occasion, we were grappling in my side yard. I was in my customary, pinned to the ground position, when the fun turned a little serious. I was irate that I couldn't free myself, and Freddy was relentless in his dominance. All the while I could hear in the background my four-legged bodyguard barking furiously. So in a moment of rage I called out for help, "KAISER!" A split second later I heard the rattle of the chain link fence, and thought, as I looked into Freddy's victorious face, "I'm about to feel sorry for you!" As you can imagine, Kaiser handled my overpowering foe with quick dispatch. A swift bite to the back, and Freddy was now the one on the ground crying. I was only eight or nine years old at the time, and I really did feel bad for my friend. I didn't like seeing Freddy hurt but at the same time it was hard not to swell with pride standing next to Kaiser like a fallen king next to his champion. Even in those days, I realized in my dog's mind he had done no wrong. To the contrary, he lived to battle dragons for his king. After putting Kaiser back in the yard, I remember walking Freddy home thinking that my dog and I were in real trouble for double-teaming him. After Freddy's mom looked at the bite marks (they were minimal because of heavy winter clothing), she had only two things to say. "Stop crying" and "You boys need to wrestle in a different yard!" This is yet another example of the nineteen-sixties mindset of "stupid kids, that's what dogs do." One lesson from these two stories might be that children shouldn't have unsupervised access to loaded guns and biting dogs.

Matthew at three years old with his best childhood friend, Kaiser at one year old

There is one other aggressive dog I can vividly recall from my oldest memories, Jingles. Jingles was a beautiful, male, rough coated Collie that cruised around the block of my childhood home on occasion. He really did jingle because of all the tags hanging on his collar, so I don't know if Jingles was his legitimate name or not, but that is how everyone in the neighborhood referred to him. He was a very friendly sort with people, but when it came to other dogs he would just as soon attack them as look at them. It's funny how certain experiences leave such a lasting impression on the human mind. That's what the sound of jingles' tags is to me, a lasting impression. I can still hear him trotting up the street and remember watching most of the loose neighbor dogs retreat for home, including Taffy. That little Cocker was tough but not stupid; she had been mauled by Jingles long ago and never forgot it. Kaiser, on the other hand loved to hear those tags jingling up the street. Thank goodness Kaiser was one of the few dogs in the area who was confined by a fence because the closer Jingles got to our end of the street, the wilder our German Shepherd became. We only had a few brief moments to get to the house and call Kaiser inside, or he would explode over the fence and take the fight directly to the collie. I remember those two dogs tangling horrifically on a few occasions. Each time the end result was the same; the Collie was running for his life towards home with Kaiser hot on his heels. There would always be at least one of us in my family (standing out in the yard for the entire world to see) futilely screaming for our dog to come home. Unlike Taffy, Jingles didn't seem to learn from the agony of defeat. After one of their encounters, we wouldn't see him for a long time. Once he healed, Jingles would return for another stab at the "king of the hill". So like an endless loop, the chaos was bound to repeat itself. The relentless pursuit of controlling territory is a powerful driving force in some dogs. When two or more dogs of this type live within the same small neighborhood (factoring in little or no handler control) battles are inevitable. Interestingly, that seemed to be of little concern to anyone in my childhood environment.

In contrast to what I outlined about yesteryear, feelings about dogs and their value appear to be much different today. Most of us would agree that today's dog owner is held to a much higher standard of responsibility and accountability. Speaking as a professional trainer and a family dog owner, I like the contemporary mindset. This modern outlook (when not taken to extremes) cultivates better living conditions for all concerned, people and dogs. With a new age of dog ownership and the responsibilities that go along with it comes a unique identity within the human- animal dynamic, the primary handler. The pivotal person and the target of this book, the primary handler, is also the most important living being in the world to a trained dog. If that is not true in your family now, it soon will be!

What makes a person a primary handler? Establishing relationship rules, supplying consequences as a result of a dog's action, enforcing parameters, and controlling the environment are all duties of a primary handler and the reasons a canine views this person as being so significant. Diligence in regards to these duties determines the importance and effectiveness of handler. Any human member of a dog's immediate family can function as a primary handler if they are willing to regularly work with their pet and are physically able to manage him. There are special requirements when considering the training of a potentially hostile dog. For example; young people (under voting age) often develop into some of our best handlers at the training center. However, when we are dealing with canine aggression, we need a person who possesses the confidence, emotional balance, and physical stature that comes with maturity. Another very important human factor that is often overlooked when training aggressive dogs is comfort. Is the family member interested in working the dog comfortable with the animal? In more cases than you can imagine, we will work with a handler who has been thrown into that position (because of available free time, let's say) even though they are scared to death of the dog. This person may have the desire and maturity to train the family pet but the anxiety that stems from their fear will cripple any attempt to communicate and direct the dog. Likewise, fondness for the animal is a requisite. You will not develop into a fair and balanced (therefore effective) handler if you can't find attributes in the canine worthy of admiration. I do realize dealing with unwanted hostile behavior is not fun, but a primary handler must learn how to manage this aspect of their pet's behavior while enjoying the multifarious, positive characteristics of the dog. A dog can accept as many primary handlers as there are members in the immediate family who are interested and capable.

Think of dog training as a relationship building process. I'm going to help you build a relationship with your pet no differently than a dancing instructor would help you develop a relationship with a new dancing partner. Learning how to tango, although a challenging dance, it is very stimulating. Effort and practice will separate the successful from the unsuccessful. When dancing, someone leads and someone follows; there is no way to lead and follow at the same time. So now is the time to decide, which role do you want? While you are making your decision, the family pet is eagerly trying to convince everyone that he was born to be a natural leader and he is up for the job. Keep in mind, the dog is going to dance with you whether you're interested or not; he was born to dance but not necessarily lead!

A police dog tracking a felon, harnessing the natural hunting drive

Rules are everything! They determine how a family or a pack operates. They define a relationship's dynamic. **Well defined rules are the first steps toward order, and order leads to peace, harmony, and health for humans and animals alike.** If you must, to organize your mind and your game plan, take several moments to sit down and write out all the aspects of your ideal (also realistic) dog and owner relationship. I actually did this with my current personal dog. He was three years old when I adopted him from a family who had been worn thin by his hostile behavior. I was most excited to get started with this fellow, but before any training began I crystallized in my mind an image of how the finished interaction would be between the two of us. A fresh, positive start was my goal, so I decided to change his name and shift the current commands he understood from German to English. On my list of "to dos" I also added about a dozen commands to my new partner's vocabulary, along with writing out a plan on how to redirect his aggressive energy. As primary handlers, we must set up a definite strategy for living with our dogs, or fuzzy rules and obscure guidelines will lead to a chaotic lifestyle and a frustrating relationship.

Rules can be as simple as don't jump into my lap without permission, or as complex as guard the door until I relieve you. In order to be meaningful to the canine student, they must be clearly understood and consistently applied. When defining the guidelines your dog should operate by, think succinct, compact, and precise. This way your companion will have little trouble comprehending the idea, and you'll have no trouble remembering every one's obligation. For example, let us consider doorway control. Doorway control for a dog can be simply conveyed as do not cross the newly exposed threshold with any part of your body without my permission. This has nothing to do with formal commands or rigid positions for the canine. The more convoluted version would involve the handler stepping back from the door before opening and calling his companion to heel then telling him to sit and stay and only then the handler would be free to return to the door and open it without the dog crossing the newly exposed threshold. I would like to interject; there is nothing wrong with the formal command approach to door control. There is simply more on the dog's and the handler's plate with this plan and that means more opportunities for a glitch. Also, if a guideline is too complicated or overly burdensome, the handler is much more likely to skip over its reinforcement when in a hurry. Think of Occam's razor when setting up your rule system. This philosophic approach briefly defined means the simplest of competing theories should be preferred to the more complex.

Supplying consequences is undoubtedly the responsibility that makes a primary handler the all-important being in the dog's eyes. All of the other responsibilities are also necessary, but the supreme authority in the family to both humans and dogs is the one who doles out consequences in connection to actions! **I cannot stress enough how important it is to allow your dog to learn through exploration.** This is the most natural form of information gathering for any canine, wild or domestic. When a dog owner affords his pet the opportunity to act and then reap the harvest of that action, he has set his pet up to learn in a meaningful way. Information gathered through an action-reaction process is information that will stick. Here's a simple mental experiment to illustrate this learning process. Imagine holding your very hungry, canine companion while he watches someone accidently (on purpose) drop their mouth-watering pork chop among a number of set mouse traps that are placed on the floor. Two feet from the mouse trap minefield is his food dish, which has just been filled with a small bit of his regular kibble. Now, without words, you could turn the quick study loose and watch how he gathers information just as nature intended. Out of habit, most dogs would run to their food dish first to gobble up the small portion of kibble, which was nothing more than a taste. After having his appetite kicked into high gear, an observant fellow would quickly move to the mouse traps where the pork chop was dropped and dive in with little hesitation. After one or two of the traps have exploded around his nose, he would more than likely fall back and assess the situation more closely. A very hungry or physically tough dog might brave the mine field another time in an attempt to appease his drive to eat. If running into exploding mouse traps was always the outcome to pursuing the pork chop, even the most determined of hungry dogs would leave someone else's treasure to rest in the minefield while he waited for more of his appropriate food, in it's appropriate place.

The obvious lesson being learned by your canine student in this experiment is that no matter how voracious the appetite, ordinary kibble in the feeding dish is enjoyable and free to eat, while someone else's pork chop, guarded by mouse traps is neither free, nor enjoyable. This experiment illustrates how quickly a dog can learn from the natural process of choosing then experiencing the connected consequences. If an exercise like this were set up in real life the canine student wouldn't require any help from the handler, or a leash, to glean all the pertinent information the experience had to offer. As a side note, a calm environment and emotionally pleasant atmosphere contribute as much to a dog's ability to absorb information as they do ours.

Now let's apply this learning approach to more practical dog training. First of all, as a primary handler (the consequence supplier), you will be the mouse trap and the feeding dish all at the same time! Let's say I'm working with a mature fox terrier who has been recently adopted into a home with a resident Siamese cat. I also want you to imagine that this fox terrier was put up for adoption because he wore down his previous family with cat chasing and squirrel killing. It would be foolish for any fox terrier owner to ignore the selectively bred background of this feisty little breed. Their inherent specialty is ridding environments of small animals. This doesn't mean every terrier is bent that way; it simply means this particular type of canine may be more inclined to subdue cats and foxes than a collie would. This predisposition to attack small animals is an important concept here, because the fox terrier I'm referring to has already proven to be a true representation of his ancestral background. This means he receives a substantial, positive charge anytime he's involved in a chase. A terrier that is inclined to work doesn't need a handler to cheer him on; the thrill of the chase and an occasional capture is all the reward he needs to be excited about work. If we add to this natural inclination a history of habitual chase and capture like I've described in this case, a real challenge lies ahead in dissuading this little guy from his self appointed and ancestral duties.

As we begin to shape this terrier's behavior by connecting consequences to decisions, we can't forget that he believes that his job is eliminating small animals, and business is good! So in order to alter the terrier's way of thinking even a little bit, we (as primary handlers) need to be impressive. In a situation like this, the deterrent for inappropriate behavior (chasing the cat) must be strong, timely, and consistent. The reward must be valuable (to the dog), timely, and consistent or there will be very little chance to get the terrier and the cat to coexist peacefully. By strong correction, I mean a non-emotional, jolting action, directed through a leash or long line attached to a Martingale, slip, or pinch collar. Often times, I find that an extended correction with a leash and slip collar is the superior method in calming a very intense canine who is already committed to his hostile aggressive action. An extended correction may be the swiftest and the safest maneuver a handler can employ when defusing canine hostility.

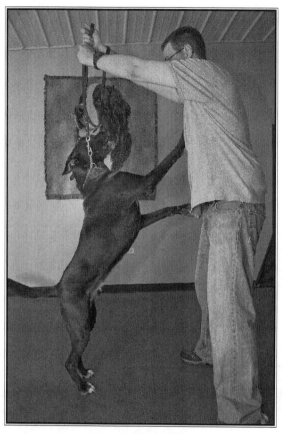

Mr. Decker having to use a leash extension to defuse Basher's aggressive challenge

Essentially, during this maneuver a handler quickly extends his arms away from the body, holding the leash shortly and securely in both hands. Ideally both hands should be held together to insure the use of both arms, and the hands (leash in grip) should be raised far enough above the floor to keep the leash taught and the dog's front toes off the ground. Correctly done, this tactic will keep the canine's mouth safely out of the reach of both the handler and the target; while at the same time remove the traction from his front feet in order to minimize his force and physicality. Even the most hostile dog held in this position for approximately ten to twenty-five seconds will become passive and quiet enough to rethink his decision. **I need to stress here, in order to reap any benefit from this action, the hostile student must be held long enough to allow the emotional hysteria to completely pass.** Once the aggressive dog settles into passivity, the handler should cautiously return his front feet to the ground and return slack to the leash, ever ready to re-extend if the canine displays further hostility.

The dog's passivity is a direct result from his feeling of ineffectiveness at controlling the environment, and his inability to gain emotional satisfaction from an aggressive surge. The extended correction should not be viewed simply as an appropriate deterrent for an inappropriate behavior, but more like a cycle halting technique which acts as a platform for redirecting a hysterical dog's focus and energy. A good analogy for this process would be the physical restraining of a young person temporarily lost in a violent tantrum. The subduing of this person should be viewed as a service of kindness that prevents possible injury to the individual and others. To help facilitate a dog's retreat into acquiescence, the handler at all times should be a master of his own emotions. There is neither room nor need for any negative emotion out of the handler during dog training, especially when dealing with aggression. Cool, calm action is what the student and the situation calls for. Hostility from the handler only fuels the already hot fire, burning in the dog.

With this extended correction technique, a handler is allowed to address an aggressive dog with dispatch, in the pertinent theater of context. This means treating the problem behavior as a whole (target or situation and the inappropriate response) and nip it in the bud, so that dog and handler can almost instantaneously move on to more positive times.

If a handler is not physically, mentally, or emotionally strong enough to use extended corrections to bring the hostile student around to focused resignation on a loose leash, then the alternative is to apply traditional leash and collar tugs but allow for more distance from the eliciting target or situation. The increased distance will reduce the effect of a target or situation and dilute a dog's emotional intensity. This, in turn, will improve the effectiveness of the less impressive leash and collar tugs. The downside to this distance approach to shaping behavior is that it requires a great deal of time to gradually work a dog into a realistic proximity of potential trouble. I have found over the past few decades that most handlers lack the necessary tenacity to carry out a distance reducing plan. Unfortunately, they give up before the consistent effort brings about their dream of hands free, command free, casual control over their dog while in proximity of potential triggers.

In some milder cases a remote control collar can be a very useful tool when refining training but a handler must remember that the mouse trap required to curb most forms of hostile expression must pack enough bite and surprise to jar the dog free from the aggressive mindset. This mindset can be almost trance like as was the case in this real fox terrier-Siamese cat situation. The instant the cat was caught in the little dog's sight, the rest of the world disappeared to the terrier. To assist in disrupting this pattern, I had the family bring the cat to each of the terrier's training sessions so we could maximize our efforts in safely teaching the little guy how to concentrate on handler wishes even though his nemesis moved about freely. Remember, a screaming or paddling style of correction only adds emotional fuel to an already raging fire and essentially works against the handler's efforts. Our overall goal in applying a deterrent or correction is to bring the dog to a calm state of mind as quickly as possible. This way the canine student will be open to handler suggestions and new ways to manage his visceral reaction to targets or situations that illicit a hostile response. **The longer the dog is allowed to dwell in an aggressive mindset, the more difficult it will be to snap him free!**

If a primary handler witnesses the dog's effort to move in the right behavioral direction (e. g. looking away from the cat as the curious creature moves into proximity) he should have something of real worth to offer him (like a special piece of food, soothing caress or genuine words of praise). If the paycheck we offer our canine student isn't of value to him, then it's also of no value in our training equation. Often times it's impossible to find a reward for the dog that is more stimulating or satisfying than the exhilarating, aggressive display itself. The main reason for meaningful deterrents is to reduce or eliminate the pleasure the dog receives from the hostile display. This way, what we have to offer as compensation for good effort will be deemed to be fair wages by the dog.

Every handler wishing to achieve equipment free, crutch free control over their dog needs to think of treats and toy rewards as a bonus not as bait. This means until the moment of delivery the treat or toy is noiseless and out of the dog's sight. Careful handling will ensure your canine student does not depend on a visual or audible crutch to pull his mind away from the target of his hostile behavior. It might be fair to say that most dog owners who are dealing with unwanted hostility in their pet would gladly agree to use bait if it helped in controlling the situation. Personally, I don't want to be saddled for the next eight to ten years with the responsibility of having, on my person, the right treat or toy to control my dog's aggression. Please don't take this last statement the wrong way. It is the rare dog I work without offering some kind of treat or toy, but I'm very careful to utilize those items only as bonuses to the physical and verbal praise. As an ideal reward system I would like the right kind of touch and the right kind of words, and there are different forms of each. For instance, soothing or stimulating touch with the appropriate inflection in the accompanying words may suffice. In each training situation covered in the following chapters, I will be very clear on how to apply the appropriate deterrent or incentive.

When defining and establishing rules for your canine companion, you are in essence setting up parameters for him to operate within. Whether they're informal, like waiting for permission to pass through a newly opened door, or formal, like holding a stay until released, if the parameter is not consistently and accurately enforced, it is truly meaningless. If guidelines on how to live are not crystal clear for your dog, he must learn to operate in a fog. How frustrating it must be to live in a pack and never figure out how to blend harmoniously! **As the primary handler, you have an obligation to keep the rules alive by supplying consequences for the dog in accordance with his cooperation or resistance to these guidelines.** Create clarity in parameters by tenaciously holding to a line you have drawn, exactly as you have drawn it. For example, if the house rule is the dog cannot cross the newly exposed threshold (as a door is opened) without permission, then don't allow him to sometimes step over the threshold with a single foot because it's only twenty-five percent of his feet. Hold to the original idea, DON'T CROSS THE NEWLY EXPOSED THRESHOLD! If you want the command "stay" (don't move until the primary handler releases you) to have real meaning for the dog then be prepared to physically replace him if he eases out of position. By the same token, if you happen to open the front door of your home and the kids with the cat charge across the threshold, but your faithful companion holds, lay on the praise! Imagine telling your very social, Golden Retriever to down and stay on the porch while you sign for a delivery package. Right in the middle of signing, the delivery man pats his leg and whistles for your companion. If your A+ student holds, walk over to him in the middle of signing and demonstrate your approval.

Enforcing parameters with a new canine student requires energy, concentration, consistency, and commitment. Deficiency in any of these areas will surely lead to deterioration of a handler's control. Supervision of behavior, supplying timely genuine praise, and administering meaningful deterrents can be a substantial drain on a person. That is why it's understandable when a dog owner says, "I had a long day at the shop and I don't feel like working with my dog right now!" At this moment, a handler has two options, either allow the canine-in-training opportunities to successfully break the team captain's clearly defined rules, or put the dog in a comfortable safe place which removes him from such an opportunity. By comfortably securing a dog any time the primary handler is unwilling or unable to enforce the rules, a pet owner is protecting the integrity of the parameters and preserving training progress in one smart move. A few suggestions for secure, comfortable, confinement include a plastic crate or wire cage of appropriate size for indoor confinement, and a covered pen or fenced yard for the outdoors. If a dog owner has the space and the inclination, a spare room could be converted into a nice pet space.

In essence, as the primary handler, what I'm suggesting you do to ensure training success is supervise the dog-in-training anytime he has freedom outside of his safe place. I also recommend that any canine student currently in training wear his training collar and leash or long line while he's being supervised. This doesn't mean the handler has to hold the leash or long line the entire time. Allow the dog to drag it around like a tail on his front end, or liken it to a man wearing a tie to work. With a little conditioning time, the collar, leash or long line will go virtually unnoticed by the dog just like part of his body. The supervision and confinement may seem demanding, but you will get used to the new routine faster than you might think. Keep telling yourself "it's not forever". I have found, after working with thousands of families and their oftentimes-challenging pets, is that after four to sixteen weeks of honest effort, that real and permanent behavior change can be observed. New habits, better decisions, and more self control on the dog's part means less energy, concentration, and commitment on the handler's part. Don't dare think that training won't start taking hold for a couple of months. Effective handling should bring about immediate, noticeable results. A few months will be required to relax the daily training regimen and deliver some freedom from equipment.

Do your best to resist any feelings of guilt that may arise over frequent confinement or equipment wearing during the initial training period. Without having the chance to meet you or your dog, simply by the fact that you're reading this book most likely your canine friend lives better than a substantial percentage of the world's human population. With all things considered (wearing a leash and collar, resting in a crate, eating once a day, and living by the new rules), your four-legged companion has better housing, diet, and health care than many people! Rest assured your pet has it made.

An integral part of a complete training regimen is controlling the environment. That means setting up the dog's living conditions so that the family dynamic and the home arrangement are conducive to positive behavior. For instance, it may be necessary to lock the front door to prevent family and friends from walking directly into a defensive dog's personal space. By locking the door the handler is afforded the opportunity to comfort his watchdog during his alarm and bring his companion into control before allowing the outsiders to enter. The primary handler's presence is crucial at this moment when guests are invited in to ensure stability and balance in the dog. The locked door ensures that the primary handler will be there. Family members who are not designated handlers should be instructed to defer to the dog's primary controller rather than trying to manage the situation themselves. If a primary handler is not available, then according to our training plan, the canine-in-training should be properly confined. Once guests have been invited in, they should be coached on how to interact with the self-controlled but defensive canine. Uneducated visitors may misinterpret the watch dog's calm demeanor and think he will be receptive to petting, when in fact he may be repulsed by the idea. A handler's job in this situation is not to give dog training instruction to the guests, but simply give out some do's and don'ts in regards to interaction with the family pet. For instance, "my watch dog needs some time to adjust to visitors so try to ignore him until I give you the green light" (a little explanation as to why is always nice). In cases involving defensive dogs, it's sometimes best for the dog's solace and/or the visitor's comfort to simply put the family pet in his safe place. With effective management of the environment, you're able to clearly demonstrate to your watchdog that the team captain is in control and that demonstration goes a long way in stabilizing aggression.

Let's consider another scenario in environmental control with a possessive, aggressive dog. Leaving multiple treasures lying about an active house, or leaving food in the feeding dish with an unsupervised, possessive canine is a disaster waiting to happen. When an innocent family member or guest walks too close to a rawhide bone or the uneaten portion of the house pet's dinner, he unwittingly triggers a possessive dog's launch into hostile action. The dog sees it as a clear threat to his cache, even though the passerby didn't notice the treasure on the way to his destination. The simple solution for this troublesome situation is to limit your loyal companion to one treasure at a time, while you're able to watch over him and immediately put it away when his interest fades. When it comes to food in the dog dish, establish one or more fifteen minute feeding periods that are supervised. If any food is left when the eating period is up, throw it out or save it for the next feeding opportunity. As always, it benefits everyone in the household to understand the rules and arrangements that have been put in place so that the rearing of the family dog is a safe and pleasurable experience.

Controlling the environment doesn't mean, as a primary handler, you have to set up a military camp. It only means tipping the scale in your favor by managing your dog's behavior through supervision, education, securing, and scheduling. I'm sure if you own an assertive dog and you've just finished reading the responsibilities of a primary handler, you must be thinking "how daunting." I can assure you after a lifetime of raising man-stopping protection dogs as family companions; the details of your duties will become so routine that the stress of raising a potentially hostile dog will seem negligible. Try not to forget that all my personal dogs were probably more aggressive than the dog you live with, yet not a single innocent person has been bitten by my dogs simply because I follow the same rules I just laid out for you. In fact, these rules were crafted from three decades of personal experience, bringing up a son and daughter around watchdogs, having family over for Thanksgiving, taking these tough guys to the park, and so forth. Provided your dog's temperament is sound (if that is in question seek out an assessment from a professional), even though he is aggressively assertive, you and those around you will be fine as long as you follow the handling advice offered in these pages and apply a healthy dose of common sense.

Assuming you have a potentially hostile or assertive dog to manage, I suggest that you invest in quality training equipment before any instruction begins. This advice really applies to any form of animal management, but it is especially important for the safety of everyone concerned (including the four legged participants) when there is an aggressive animal to be handled. Try not to think "pretty" or "trendy" when buying a leash or collar. Instead, think of dependable, secure, and ergonomic. The substance of the equipment selected should match the size of the dog in training. Don't settle for a leash in a pet store simply because it sports an appealing logo. If it doesn't fit your dog then it's not appealing. You may have to refuse a free hand-me-down collar from your brother because it's not the appropriate weight for your companion. Trying to make do with inferior equipment will usually come back to haunt you!

The minimum dog training tools include a basic four to six foot long obedience leash with a safety snap at one end and a generous, well stitched handle at the other (please, no extra loops, rings, snaps or stool bags attached); an indestructible nylon or chain slip collar which allows for a close but comfortable fit over the dog's head (no logging chains or barge ropes); a long nylon line of approximately fifteen to thirty feet in length (a half inch to one inch in width depending on the size of the dog), again with a single safety snap at one end and a well stitched handle at the other; a leather or nylon open mouth, full cheek coverage, long wearing muzzle with an adjustable neck and nose strap (the appropriate length and width to match the dog's head size is critical for this piece of equipment) and a comfortable, escape proof, bed size crate for indoor confinement (baby gates across open doorways don't accomplish the same thing). A nice option is an escape proof containment system outside, like a securely fenced backyard, or a sturdy, welded wire pen, or a chain link dog run (unfortunately, electronic signal fences don't count because we can't afford a break in electric current and we must be able to keep outsiders out with a tangible barrier). If temporarily anchoring a dog with a tether is ever necessary, utilize a substantial buckle collar for this purpose and not a working slip collar. The buckle collar is also the appropriate collar to hang tags. When selecting your training equipment is there is no room for anything coming apart, breaking off, or getting out. When safety is on the line, purchase quality products that fit! As the training scenarios unfold with each chapter, I will describe the equipment needed to manage a dog in that particular situation and how to utilize it most effectively.

To muzzle or not to muzzle is a reasonable question. A reasonable answer is absolutely use a muzzle, even if there is only a remote chance that your dog may bite another living being. What's wrong with a comfortable open mouth muzzle after all? Probably only the inappropriate stigma attached to it. A muzzle stigma exists only in the minds of uninformed people, so it shouldn't matter to you what they think about your muzzle wearing companion. I have found over the years that the moment an assertive dog is fitted with a muzzle, everyone around that animal relaxes and this in turn relaxes the dog. So this one piece of equipment, all on its own, breaks a negative cycle of tension-reaction-heightened tension-heightened reaction that leads to more and more explosive encounters between a hostile dog and his targets. Once the cycle has been broken, whether it be by a muzzle or effective leash and collar action, an opportunity has been created to activate a new cycle that runs more like this: difficult self restraint-partial calmness-easy self restraint-complete calmness and this cycle leads in turn to genuine harmony (not fondness) between an aggressive dog and his targets.

Fold the straps back and put the food into the muzzle before presenting it to the dog

Give the dog a chance to zero in on the food

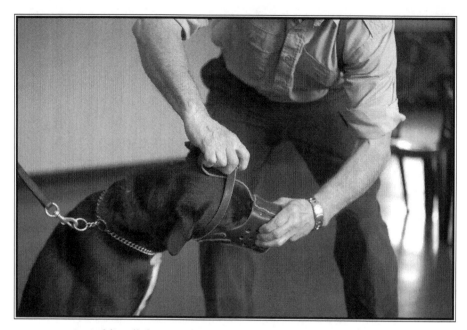

Smoothly pull the straps over his head while he's enjoying the treat

A muzzle is an absolutely essential piece of equipment if a canine student has directed strong protest toward his primary handler. It really doesn't matter why a dog uses aggression against his handler, and I've heard every imaginable reason why somebody's dog was "justified" in doing so. Any hostility must be quashed. I can tell you from experience, dealing calmly and deftly with a dog who's trying to bite you is a challenge. The muzzle affords a handler the luxury of protection, which removes a handler's need for retreat or explosive action. It also eliminates panic. This in turn allows for the necessary time to manage an assertive dog effectively. Demonstrating to an aggressive canine a strong, steady demeanor shows that you are unaffected by his challenge. This does a lot in removing value from a potentially important tool of his. You should also keep in mind the muzzle helps in preventing you from fueling the aggressive fire with your own intense emotion. That is that's one of the keys to training success.

If your potentially aggressive dog is muzzled when he's exposed to outsiders, you deserve a pat on the back for being a responsible, courteous and rational owner who's more concerned with the welfare of others than with appearances. The muzzle helps you shield people and other animals from potential injury that they may have brought on by over stepping boundaries or by ignoring interaction rules you put in place for safety reasons. There's no shame in owning a dog that may bite. I've never lived with a dog that wouldn't bite under certain conditions. All my canine companions are conditioned to wearing a muzzle from the very beginning of handling, just like they're accustomed to a collar and crate. My dogs are first introduced to the muzzle as a treat dispenser. Literally, for days when I present the muzzle to my new student, I say "muzzle". The dog will reach all the way into the nose piece and retrieve a bit of food placed there. After a week's worth of training like this, a stranger can silently present the muzzle to my dog and be hard pressed to keep my companion's nose out of it. During the second week of conditioning, I begin fastening the neck strap around my dog and sooth him while he wears it for just a few moments. Importantly, the entire time I hold him securely by the collar. I will not allow any struggling with the muzzle in an attempt to remove it. In the third and final week of conditioning the few moments of wear turns into long minutes while walking on leash, all the while soothing and preventing any attempts he may make at removing the equipment. Wearing a muzzle can become as comfortable as wearing a collar. Time in the muzzle is what makes the difference. This is no different than donning eye glasses for the first time. During the first few days of wearing new eye glasses it's difficult to see past the frames, but as the days roll by the frames completely disappear (I delve into more conditioning details in Chapter ten).

Comfortable confinement, what a relief! Can you imagine owning a horse without a barn, a turtle without a terrarium, or a human child without a crib, playpen, baby gates, or car seat? Most people accept the idea of proper confinement in these cases. However, there are countless dog owners who don't acknowledge the same advantages to confining their canine family members. In fact, a true aversion to canine confinement exists in many households. After thirty-one years in the dog training business, I still find that mindset hard to explain. I would speculate, based on thousands of client comments, that the aversion to confining the family dog stems from an anthropomorphic empathy that is compounded by an owner's view of their pet as an innocent free spirit. It's relatively easy to comprehend how someone could imagine being confined like their dog (anthropomorphizing), or attribute a spritely aspect to their life loving companion. For me, the challenge in appreciating this view is that it usually only applies to Canis familiaris and not to a spouse in a cubical, a baby in a crib, or a horse in a stall. So don't let guilt get in the way of responsible confinement. The benefits of psychological calming, training success, and neighborhood harmony far outweigh any negatives that could stem from comfortable canine containment.

No matter how well trained my dogs become; I regularly make use of indoor crates and outdoor pens. My companions are much too valuable to me to head out on the road without having them secured in their crates in the back of my truck. I would love to be able to spend all day, every day outside with my dogs burning up energy. But that's not possible, and I have to spend the lion's share of my waking hours taking care of duties just like you. Whenever possible, I'll put my two German Shepherds outside in their pens to enjoy the fresh air like I wish I could. When I have gatherings at my home, there will be on regular occasion someone who is uncomfortable around my formidable dogs. Out of courtesy I will tuck my companions into their comfortable condos (crates with bedding and chewing bone) until the situation has changed. Sometimes I put my dogs away for their own sake (e.g., a house full of young 'ns wearing my four legged monsters out with "bring this" and "catch that"). I will reiterate here, without proper confinement for your dog, complete training success is almost out of reach. **We'll exit this topic with two new mantras, "containment is good" and "structure is healthful".**

Chapter Three

Dog Against Dog Aggression

My two adult male, intact, German Shepherds live peacefully with me at home. Harmony exists between the two assertive males for a couple of reasons. First and most importantly, at the earliest moment in forming a relationship with them I established myself as team captain by setting policies and by supplying consequences in connection with their actions. The consequences they quickly learned were consistent, timely, and meaningful. My response to their behavior could range from upbeat and stimulating to soothing or neutral, and if necessary a serious or businesslike approach. What became evident to my dogs right away was this guy sets schedules, designates boundaries and doles out consequences; he must be the captain of our team.

This relationship was first established with each dog as individuals and then later adjusted to accommodate the boys as a pair. The reward for all this effort is that both dogs automatically defer to me, not to each other. They maintain a high level of self control over their drive and energy, and they both are able to think very clearly about rules even though they are caught in a whirlwind of activity. The bottom line is Hector and Ivan are in a habit of considering me before anyone or anything else; this means they can't get carried away obsessing over one another and where they stand in each other's eyes. The three of us make up a pack. We operate by the rules I put in place. We all understand and are comfortable with this family dynamic, that's what makes us insiders and everyone else outsiders. This pack concept makes up the second reason my two German Shepherds live so comfortably together. They are "everyday" familiar with one another, and they know what to expect from each other in every situation. They don't feel that way about any other dog. So even though Hector and Ivan compete with one another, it's safe competition within the parameters their team leader set up.

Now let's consider outsiders, which could be any living being not a part of the immediate family group. Our prime concern in this chapter will be canine outsiders that instinctively represent a prime challenge to pack longevity. The non-pack member canine is competing for exactly the same resource that the defending group depends on, unlike a bear or a human who have significantly different needs than the dog group. Since Canis familiaris (our familiar canine) is a pack mentality animal like his predecessor Canis lupus, a dog thinks in terms of insiders and outsiders. Dogs need a pack or family arrangement in order to flourish, and only a finite number will fit in any given pack. With wild canines, pack membership means survival because multiple individuals are needed to secure territory, to aid in the rearing of pups, and to team up in the capture of large game. Only an optimal number of pack members will work. This optimal number is not a fixed value. Pack size is similar to determining the size of a human, immediate family. The average number of individuals who make up a family will vary from time to time, but in essence we're looking at a group made up of a breeding pair, a juvenile or two from a previous breeding, several pups from a recent litter, and maybe an uncle or aunt who fits in pretty well. If a canine family has too many members, securing enough territory to feed everyone becomes impractical and there may be more pups whelped than can be sustained. Rank and order also becomes a more challenging issue for larger family groups including man and beast (there never seems to be a shortage of chiefs or an abundance of workers in any social arrangement). I'm sure most of us would agree, someone needs to be in charge and the rest of the crowd willing to follow in order for a group to function. The truth is, as membership increases, the likelihood that this kind of arrangement can be maintained decreases.

Reviewing the reasons why most canines thrive in modest size packs, but only get by in oversized groups, may strike many of you as "so what". It must be emphasized that we may have removed our pet from the wild, but we haven't removed all the wild from our pet. Even though our family canine cannot cognize why, he instinctively knows outsiders trying to make their way into the pack or pack territory are disrupting the natural balance of pack dynamics. Dogs can view other dogs as the most potent outside challenge to peace and prosperity (as compared to humans or other animals for example) because of an instinctual template, which is evolution's guide to what is and isn't important. Survival of a species depends on family unit survival, which means being able to produce offspring and see them into adulthood. In the case of our domestic dog, he is instinctually compelled to do his part in carrying out this biological plan. That's why he may be willing to patrol territory, guard his portion of sustenance, copulate if the right things are in place, and protect the pups to ensure his family's characteristics are perpetuated. Seen from a canine's perspective which has been influenced from countless generations of experiences, no animal can interfere with maintaining the family's genes like another canine that is competing for exactly the same niche with exactly the same plan for spreading his family's genes.

Matthew managing Yogi while Ivan catches a ball

Before I launch into the management of dog on dog aggression, I want to outline additional common aspects of this potent challenger threat. Some dog aggressive dogs behave so as a pre-emptive measure brought on by one or more unprovoked attacks from the past. After a couple of rough encounters at the park, even a relatively passive canine may establish a pattern of being on red alert, always on the lookout for incoming threats, and ever ready to flip the pre-emptive aggression switch. Once a dog becomes red alert prone, even an innocent approach from an energetic, gregarious dog may trigger a hostile response, which in turn sets in motion an aggressive pattern in the onetime innocent, albeit intense canine visitor.

Let's take, for example, a frequent case at my training center. A five month old pit bull puppy was rescued from a less than desirable home where dog sparring was encouraged. Although this particular pup has never received nor initiated a hostile attack, he tends to be intensely attracted to other dogs due to a predisposition that stems from many generations of selectively breeding one top dog fighter with another. No different than breeding a top herding Border Collie with another to increase the likelihood of the ensuing litter yielding a top herding dog. As a side note here, simply because a dog has been selectively bred to perform a task, this doesn't mean he's destined for this line of work. A primary handler is more than capable of encouraging or discouraging inherent tendencies in their companion. Being aware of a dog or breed's tendencies and predispositions does greatly aid in forming a successful training plan, no differently than accurately assessing and managing your own strengths and weaknesses leads to a fruitful life path. When this happy, dog intense, pit bull puppy charges a red alert dog with the intentions of wrestling only, it's not uncommon for a red alert dog to interpret the forceful and physical charge as hostile and respond with his own defensive and sometimes painful response which in turn may bring out an aggressive retaliation from the puppy. It doesn't take but one or two of these experiences to establish a more forceful approach in our bold, sparring minded puppy. Since charging a competitor in fun to wrestle sometimes ends in a more serious battle, then cut to the chase and charge in to fight to keep a slight advantage. One might reason at this point why would the pup charge in at all; the answer is twofold, the inherent irresistible urge to be dog intense and the energy rush associated with hostile display along with the stimulation of competition itself.

In each of these cases, a Pack Minded individual, a Red Alert canine and a Bold Wrestler, the dog on dog aggression did not stem from an inherent dislike or aversion to other dogs. Stimulation is the usual culprit, excitement over an immediate challenge or perceived threat heightens the senses and it doesn't seem to matter whether a dog is an instigator or recipient, the juices are flowing. This is why the solution to most hostile situations is not to develop more dog fondness through excessive social contact with other canines. The solution I have found to be most effective in mitigating this intense behavior is to promote indifference in regards to other dogs; that is, reduce a dog's interest in other canines through effective handling and environmental control. Exposure to other dogs is absolutely critical during the mitigating process. We must repeatedly demonstrate to the dog hostile canine that focusing or concentrating on other dogs only leads to negative consequences and indifference leads to reward. Keep in mind, socializing with or exposure to other canines has nothing to do with physical contact. Physical contact with other dogs invariably lends itself to stronger attraction and the likelihood of threatening or unpleasant posturing. If we are considering the average family dog, he has ample opportunity to affectionately or playfully interact with other members of his pack whether that be humans or animals. Since we are concerned with the domestic dog, it needs to be stated that all his social needs can be met by humans in the absence of other canines and that is the beauty of domestication.

Creating a feeling of indifference toward the intended target is the only way to build lasting control over hostility in the dog-aggressive dog. My strategy for building this self control in the aggressive dog is relatively straight forward. Like paddling directly up stream to reach a safe landing, I utilize a balance of deterrents and rewards to take away attractiveness from the canine target and redirect it to the handler. I will also describe a second path to the same destination, which is analogous to a long portage over challenging terrain. In the second scenario the use of deterrents are minimized, but the time and distance required to neutralize the target are greatly increased.

Either route gets you to the landing; it's really a matter of personal preference as to which one you choose. I will remind you throughout this book that there are usually numerous ways to manage a behavior shaping task, and I hope to outline a couple of approaches that have proven to be successful in each training section.

The first step in desensitizing a dog-aggressive dog toward his intended target is to recognize and disrupt a self rewarding, behavioral chain of events. Let's walk through a behavioral sequence common with a Pack Minded dog. The usual catalyst would be a strange dog approaching our canine student's territory, pack proximity (if away from home), or personal space. If our canine student perceives this intruder as a threat (to pack harmony or resources), he will respond with hostility in order to eliminate or run off the threat. Regardless of the turnout to the hostile encounter (either the canine student or intruder is eliminated or run off), our dog will experience temporary relief from intruder challenge. With our dog's primitive mind, an easy connection can be made in the chain of events: intruder creates stress- hostile canine student display—rush of energy and excitement—and lastly relief of stress. With this kind of association, it's easy to understand how a behavior pattern is so easily established, because for our dog-aggressive dog it is very simple: target—expression—satisfaction. Now it may not be such a stretch to understand why dog-aggressive dogs almost hope for the appearance of a target and the opportunity to express, excite, and experience satisfaction.

The expectations and the sequence of events are nearly the same with the other two dog aggressive personality types I referred to as Red Alert and Bold Wrestler. In the case of our Red Alert dog, a chain of events may go as follows; the appearance of a potentially threatening canine—our student's pre-emptive hostile display—a rush of energy and excitement—and the end of the impending danger. This could be summarized as: target—expression—satisfaction. In the case of our Bold Wrestler, the sequence could manifest as: the appearance of a challenger –an aggressive charge into action—a rush of energy and excitement—challenger dominated. Just like in the other cases the sequence is: target—expression—satisfaction.

Training success depends entirely on disrupting the chain of negative events at the earliest possible link. The primary link we are looking for is our canine student's intense focus on another dog. It really doesn't matter why our dog in training is concentrating on a canine target; we need to redirect his focus as soon as possible, and the best place for a dog's focus is on the handler. In order to accomplish this challenging task, as the primary handler (consequence supplier), we must demonstrate to our student that negative consequences will be connected to intense dog focus. We also need to associate attention toward handler with pleasant consequences, especially in the presence of potential canine targets. Along with these standard behavior shaping duties, the handler of a dog-aggressive dog needs to convey to his companion that all canine competition and incoming threats will be managed or neutralized by the team leader (the handler). To truly extinguish this type of hostility a dog-aggressive dog must get used to standing down (deferring to the handler). The dog must be able to resist self preservation urges (energy and drive control), and he must be able to think clearly in the real world (mindfulness in the thick of distraction). These are the same relationship aspects that represent any successful dog training activity. The real challenge with aggression control cases is being able to build and sustain this kind of a relationship within the proximity of intense or threatening competition. The first step in managing hostile canine behavior is to thoroughly develop manners and formal command response in your dog away from the hostile targets if at all possible. Give yourself and your companion a chance to shoulder these relationship responsibilities before putting them to the test in a hostile situation.

Before I set the training stage I'm going to make a few assumptions. First, the dog in training is physically and psychologically healthy. Second, the handler is physically and psychologically healthy. Third, the necessary quality equipment is readily available. Lastly, the space needed for training is secured and the canine student has had preliminary basic obedience instruction as I outline in "The Ten Natural Steps To Training The Family Dog". Now let's set up a training environment around observation, timing, distance, and intensity. In order to recognize the first link in a hostile chain of events (the canine student's focus on a canine target), the handler needs to be prepared to concentrate primarily on his dog in training. That's why a public park is not an ideal place to begin training, although it is the appropriate place to finish it. There are too many unpredictable variables at the park as well as an overload of distractions for both the handler and a new canine student. At my training center I arrange the instruction environment so that the choice target enters the scene at a prescribed time and place. I make sure with a new dog-in-training that extraneous distractions are minimized, and the canine target remains at a safe yet engaging distance. I do my best to select a target that will be stimulating but not overwhelming. I see to it that the target's handler has absolute control over his dog and is well instructed on his role in the training scenario. All this planning allows the handler of the dog- in-training to concentrate on one thing, HIS DOG. This way, we significantly increase the handler's odds of spotting the first reaction in the hostile chain of events, and this ability dramatically improves the likelihood of training success.

A canine student's commitment towards a target is your call to action. That commitment is the first link in the negative chain. That is the initial behavior the handler should recognize. It's OK if your dog visually checks on another canine in his area or casts his nose into the breeze to catch a whiff of the stranger. Think of commitment as directed energy such as: deliberate movement towards an outsider, posturing (standing rigid, baring teeth, raising a stiff tail or bristling) in the direction of another dog, or staring or vocalizing (barking, growling or whining) at the competition. In truth, I want my personal dog to be fully aware of what's going on in his environment. I just don't want him getting carried away with excessive dog interest. If a person were able to witness the first spark leaping from the fire pit onto the forest floor, they could abate an impending inferno with a single, wet finger tip. If however, the spark went unnoticed even for a moment, significant amounts of water would be needed to douse the flames. If the flames weren't immediately attended to, fire fighters and helicopters would be required to battle the blaze. So it is exactly the same with canine aggression, watch for the initial spark!

One of the most dog hostile dogs I've ever worked with is my current personal companion, Hector. He is a seventy pound German shepherd out of European working lines. When I took him on as a training project and a possible companion, he was three years old and absolutely full of himself. Although his original family had raised him from a puppy and loved him very much, they could not deal with his dog aggressive behavior. The first time I met Hector he had several drains hanging from his neck and shoulders as a result of a dog fight with his brother (that was owned by another family member). This happened to be the last straw for Hector's family; they could not understand how he could be so hostile with a dog with whom he had grown up with. I remember them asking me what went wrong because "they used to play so well together." My response was relatively succinct, and I'm afraid not very comforting. I told them nothing went wrong; many light hearted puppies grow into serious minded adults and natural puppy wrestling turns into natural adult fighting. In their defense, Hector did come from a long line of very serious working dogs. They were trying to manage a wheel barrow full of drive, energy, and physicality, and the handlers were simply worn down. I could see why they threw in the towel after three years of ownership.

At the time of this writing, I have owned Hector for eighteen months. He assists me when I work with dog-aggressive dogs by being an animated, confident, and intense target. When he helps me, he does so with no assistance from another handler or a leash. He will work or play as close to the challenger (that's secured in my hands) as I need with almost no concern on his part over the canine student's hostility. Hector is the dog I can count on to keep his cool in the face of genuine threat from a client's dog. His is a remarkable story of energy and drive redirection, handler devotion, and distraction management. This incredible, behavioral turnaround is due mostly to his outstanding and inherent, working potential, in other words, his ability to learn and adapt with gusto allowed me (over a period of many months) to shape his character strengths into honest working skills.

Hector, looking back at the camera, peacefully enjoying the company of dogs

Hector's original family erroneously thought he was born with a defective personality, when in truth he was simply born with a lot of personality. In order to significantly alter Hector's behavior, I had to tap into his inherent training abilities (high intelligence, willingness to please, retention of information, and quick recovery from negative learning experience) while executing an effective training plan. It was also of paramount importance that I maintained a structured environment over an extended period of time. **I want to stress here, his personality did not and will not change. For better or worse, my dog and your dog came into to this world with the temperament and disposition they will go out with.** No matter how hard we train, we're not going to change what our dog is; we can only adjust how he behaves. That is why it so important to pick out a dog for the family that is actually suited for that particular lifestyle, or else you will spend years trying to fit your canine square peg into the family round hole. This was exactly the case with Hector; good people and a good dog don't always make a good fit. In regards to this case, I'm really not that special. I'm just a better fit for Hector, and that's why this story has such a happy ending (it doesn't hurt that I've spent the last thirty years working with dogs like him).

Hector's training path was like paddling straight up stream, after several weeks of bonding and light handling (purposefully avoiding any negative, behavioral issues); I jumped right into his major negative issue, dog hostility. In reality there was no way to completely avoid the issue, because his focus on other dogs nearly ruined every positive experience I tried to set up. Working with an explosive dog like Hector afforded only a fraction of a moment between seeing another dog and committed rage. With such a tiny window of opportunity for pre-emptive handler action, redirecting focus, or preventing a hostile fire by snuffing a seminal spark was nearly impossible.

Knowing Hector's ability to adeptly respond to a full range of formal commands, and knowing how manageable he already was with moderate distractions, I purposely introduced dogs into his immediate training area and handled the situation like every other distraction conditioning session. The biggest difference with working Hector around dogs as compared to other distractions (like people, food or cats) was his intensity. His attraction and reaction to other dogs was exponentially more powerful. To Hector, canine outsiders represented a class of distractions that were separate from everything else in this physical world. He was an entirely different dog to handle when other canines (even passive, young or old ones) were present. When another dog stepped into his environment, in less than a second, my happy, eager to please companion turned into a mindless, numb, and hysterical monster. However, the potency of a canine target and the strength of Hector's reaction did not necessitate a change in the distraction conditioning plan (which is essentially removing importance from the distraction or target while adding importance to the primary handler simultaneously).

What needs to be done is simple, albeit challenging in an extreme case like this. First, the handler needs to lessen the value of distractions through neutralization. Secondly, the handler needs to increase his own value (as measured by his canine partner) through stimulation. In order to neutralize a distraction, a canine student's commitment towards the target needs to be associated with a negative consequence like a leash and collar tug (the potency of the negative consequence should correlate to the might of the student's commitment). In Hector's situation this amounted to strong, repeated leash and collar jolts just to curb his hysteria, leaving alone the idea of redirecting his focus. Only after numerous repetitions of quashing Hector's hysteria over a canine target was I able (in a slightly calmer atmosphere) to work on redirecting his focus.

Bringing Hector's attention around to me (his new team leader) was significantly easier than dousing his hysteria towards other dogs. Even though the process was the same, I didn't need nearly the force or repetition in leash and collar action to be effective. This turn of focus from target to handler also allowed me to genuinely reward Hector for his efforts of self control, and that began a new, positive trend of training while in the company of other dogs. Until this shift in Hector's attention occurred, there was little chance to offer him anything stimulating or positive during training after the appearance of a canine target. In his mind nothing compared in value to the competing dog and the exhilaration he experienced in addressing the outsider. I also had to be very careful not to add more energy to an already boiling situation. That's why from the very beginning of Hector's training, value needed to be obliterated in the canine target through the association between his commitment to the outsider and negative consequences. Only after devaluing the canine targets was I able to build up importance in me through the association of attention to the handler and positive consequences. Keep in mind, in order to neutralize the competition for Hector, not only did I have to supply negative consequences for focus on the target, I also had to make sure that another dog could not make successful advances on us and become a physical interference. The only way to make sure that wouldn't happen was to work with a canine target that was competently handled on leash or secured in an enclosure, and that's precisely what I did. Trying to work with a dog-aggressive dog out in the open neighborhood or at a park is seldom a good idea, at least not until you've reached the final stage of training which is the proofing process.

Once the commitment to a target has been quashed through effective deterrent, a handler needs to engage his dog calmly by calling his name and rewarding a positive response with praise, a little play or food. Our goal in this kind of training scenario is to create a slightly stimulating aura around the handler which attracts our dog's attention naturally and positively. Another choice of engagement is giving your dog a light or simple directive that allows for easy success, and of course a reward for proper follow through. If your canine student is unwilling to respond to these handler engagement opportunities because he's still too committed to the distraction, deliver another training collar action with increased sharpness and repeat the engagement attempts until you feel his focus towards the target has been disrupted. Remember, during this entire process the distraction remains within the immediate training environment. The canine distraction must be part of the training environment (a manageable distance from the dog-in-training) in order to convey these all important ideas to the student. First, the distraction should not be more attractive than the handler. Second, a canine student's responsibilities don't change because an outsider dog is present. Third, the dog-in-training is unable to agitate the canine target in any way. Fourth, a canine distraction will not be allowed to engage a canine student. The very moment your dog buys into these four truths, all his dog aggression issues are under control. **As I mentioned earlier, with Hector or any new dog I take on (regardless of age), I spend a period of time (about a month) establishing a light and positive relationship before ever attempting to tackle a behavioral problem.**

I chose a direct training route to manage Hector's aggressive behavior rather than an often used indirect approach, because an indirect approach to neutralizing a target requires considerably more distance (between student and target) and substantially more repeated experiences over a longer period of time. The actual plan for a circuitous, distraction conditioning route begins with a canine student far enough away from the outsider dog that leash and collar action would not be needed to quash hysteria or redirect attention to the handler. The only things needed to raise the handler's attractiveness above that of the distraction is stimulation from the team leader in the way of communication, play or treats. With this indirect approach to neutralization, distance from the target is the critical ingredient. Be aware, there is a direct correlation between the aggression intensity of a student and the distance needed to afford a successful training experience. Given Hector's extreme personality, trying to arrange enough buffer area to allow another dog to enter the training scene neutrally would be very challenging. Regardless of the safe distance needed at the beginning of instruction, whenever the dog-in-training demonstrates responsiveness to handler with no concern over canine distractions, reduce the area between student and target just enough to create a new but manageable challenge. Over time and after many repetitions, the canine student draws within a normal social range of his competition and is able to function without hostile expressions.

Taking a more circuitous training route much like an overland portage (rather than paddling straight up stream) would have consumed months of Hector's working life. It would have also been very difficult to execute because of the extreme distance from a target that would have been needed to initiate training in a neutral mindset. Like every other dog-aggressive dog, Hector saw canine outsiders as a potential battle he needed to gear up for; and as I described earlier, it doesn't matter what the trigger is for the aggressive rush, expressing hostility is exhilarating. So in Hector's case (an intense combination of Pack Minded, Bold Wrestler, and Red Alert behavior) any dog of any kind within fifty to seventy-five yards was a call to arms and an instant explosion into rage. Think of this distance as his personal bubble or buffer zone. In his highly alert mind, if a canine outsider penetrated this space, it was clearly viewed (by him) as an infraction and action was required. With the indirect portage route to de-sensitization, the target needs to first appear to the dog-in-training far enough away that even though an outsider, there is enough distance to mitigate any perceived challenge or threat. Here in lies the training challenge with many dogs including my dog Hector. How does a handler arrange such a buffer zone with dogs that have such far reaching radar?

In my dog's case, I wasn't exaggerating about the fifty to seventy five yards of surveillance radius. In order to expose my dog passively to another canine, I would have to initiate Hector's training at a distance greater than half the length of a football field from any canine target. It doesn't take much imagination to grasp the difficulty of this challenge. If I were able to arrange this set up over and over again without the interference of an unplanned dog wandering into the training arena, my plan would be to grab Hector's attention in a positive fashion such as calling his name. When he responds, offer him praise, a toy, or food reward. Alternatively, I may give him a simple command (that lends itself to success), and then follow his successful response with the same kind of rewards. When (notice I didn't use if!) a dog fails to respond to the cue or directive, the handler should utilize leash and collar tugs to grab the dog's attention and immediately offer another chance at success by repeating the cue or command. Of course if your dog is responsive the second time around, pay him with rewards as if the first failed attempt never occurred. If the canine student fails to redirect his attention towards the handler a second time, repeat the process and keep repeating until success is reached. Employ all of your focus and patience with this training plan. Persistence is important, but so is positivity. Once your companion has mastered self control and responsiveness at this safe distance (regardless of how many training sessions it may take), encourage the target to move in close enough to generate attractiveness. Repeat the entire process of desensitizing until close, real life encounters with other dogs are manageable.

The body language from both dogs clearly signals to the other, "I don't want to play"

This plan should be initiated the very moment the dog-in-training notices the canine target, regardless of how he picks up on the presence of the other dog (through his eyes, ears or nose). The idea is to convince our dog (over time and through experience) that outsider dogs at the appropriate distance represent no challenge or threat, and they are not nearly as exhilarating or important as the primary handler. Because we initiate this indirect distraction conditioning plan at such a great distance from the target, we essentially begin the process with far less intensity in regards to attraction and reaction. It seems on the surface to be the most positive approach since there is less deterrent and more reward from the start, The down side is in the difficulty of setting up enough safe buffer zone (between the dog-in-training and the target) and allowing enough time to gradually work the target closer and closer to real life proximity while preserving our canine student's composure and handler focus.

Regardless of how you go about distraction desensitization, a handler needs to be careful not to be caught off guard. The frequency of an experience will reinforce a dog's appropriate or inappropriate behavior depending on the outcome of that experience. It is critical that the primary handler control the environment during the training process, be prepared to manage the dog in the event of unexpected appearances by canine outsiders, and see to it that your dog responds as he should so he learns the desired lesson. Keep in mind, it really doesn't matter whether you choose a direct or indirect route to controlling your companion's dog aggression. **The final goal is the suppression of the canine student's hostility through self control, not through commands or restraints.**

Although the opponent is passive, it doesn't mitigate the aggressor's intensity

For all the readers that may be witnessing dog intense behavior in their young canine companions, the next paragraphs are for you. I have another dog that lives with me, his name is Ivan, and he's Hector's nephew. Cut from the same genetic cloth as his uncle, he's a combination of impressive traits: high energy + obsessive drive + confidence. Ivan was the second pick out of a litter of six. I knew his parents well, having worked with both of them through obedience and protection training. I also had the opportunity to work with four additional pups from that litter (all in different homes).

Early on Ivan showed signs of significant dog intensity (before sixteen weeks), and he was on the fast track to developing into his dog-aggressive uncle. In truth, this common thread of dog hostile behavior ran through Ivan's entire clan. Ivan has just turned eighteen months old at the time of this writing and is well into his career of bed bug detection. Training him to be a detection dog was a cakewalk, given his inherent working potential; however, preparing him for the myriad of search environments that he would be exposed to was the real challenge. Comprehending how to crawl into this or climb over that seemed natural to Ivan, but ignoring the presence of other dogs required real effort on his part.

As I've described ad nauseam by now, dog training is a team function, and it seldom gets better than building a team from scratch. Unlike his uncle who came to me with three years of baggage and various habits (some good and some not so good), Ivan was a clean slate at only nine weeks old when I took him home. This meant the bulk of his training was accomplished through the pleasant and gradual process of desirable habit building. With such a young pup, there are no old, undesirable habits to quash before the development of new ones. Training with a pup begins by imprinting ideas through stimulating interaction, as one would do during game play. Guiding, encouraging, and accompanying, are the primary obligations of a puppy trainer. Deterring and discouraging are still necessary with even the youngest of canine students, but only in a light or nurturing fashion. So in the seminal moments of Ivan's training, I created games for "find this", "come to me", "jump on that", and "go there". I also had to use puppy size leash and collar actions to discourage him from grabbing my granddaughter's sandwich and to deter him from thinking too much about other dogs.

Ivan's canine, distraction conditioning began the first afternoon I brought him home. He had to acclimate to living in close proximity to his uncle that wouldn't tolerate nursing like his mother did or bullying like his littermates did. I want to interject a very important thought here. It was not, and I'll repeat, it was not Hector's job to teach Ivan. I never allowed Hector the freedom to control Ivan, and I never gave Ivan the freedom to harass Hector. **Policy making is the primary handler's duty. Discouraging and reinforcing behaviors are the primary handler's responsibilities, and that was all up to me.** Hector was special to Ivan because he was a canine insider, he was one of the pack, and part of our family's dynamic, but he was not the alpha. Ivan comprehended and accepted quickly (within days), that his uncle was neither threatening competition nor was he the team leader, and this understanding became an integral part of our relationship foundation.

From this standpoint, Ivan began forming his opinion of other dogs and their importance in relation to mine. Although he had the genetic predisposition to grow into a dog intense fellow, I began altering this course the first afternoon he came to live with me. Shifting importance from Hector to me was a critical first step in this process, as was introducing task oriented games for drive and energy channeling. The natural next step in Ivan's puppy training was outlining how to manage both human and canine outsiders. Given the tender age and clean slate of my new pup, I chose the indirect route to distraction conditioning.

The Portage approach was easy to set up for ten week old Ivan. I didn't need half a football field of buffer distance to begin training like I did with Hector. I also had no hysteria to deal with when he did become interested in an approaching outsider, so taking the fun out of reacting to the target was easy (just a few light leash tugs). Redirecting Ivan's focus towards me was even easier. Since he was so young, life hadn't become so serious yet. As far as he was concerned, intruders were actually adult dog considerations as it would have been for him in a wild situation. Since there was no real history of interaction with outside competition in Ivan's life yet, outsiders were more of a curiosity than anything else. Pulling his attention away from dogs was as simple as presenting a toy or treat. Even the excited utterance of his new name would bring him around to full focus.

Without the history of experience and without the serious perspective of an adult, Ivan only felt hints of hostility or competiveness towards outsiders. The distance I needed to begin his dog distraction conditioning was a mere five yards, so it was very easy to arrange unlike the cumbersome fifty yards required for his uncle. In the event of an unexpected intruder, I could quickly whisk Ivan up into my arms and deal with the intruder, without explosion of violence. Working with a malleable, receptive puppy also means minimal repetitions. I didn't have much to prove here, Ivan had already accepted that I was the team leader and he was actually relieved that he had someone to follow and model after. When I began training Hector, he was reeling from three years of successfully challenging the rules and he had to be convinced that history was not going to repeat itself. Showing Ivan a few times how our team dealt with outside competition at a given distance was as good as gospel as far as he was concerned. The process of moving the target ever closer to the pup-in-training was expeditious to say the least. I was careful in Ivan's training to expose him little by little to ever more intense dog personalities.

Just as it should be done with your pet, begin dog distraction conditioning with mild or easily controlled canine personalities at first, and then gradually increase the intensity of the target as your student demonstrates the appropriate deftness.

Today, Ivan brushes past (actually bumps into routinely) strange dogs so effortlessly during work and play that a spectator would swear he has no sight or sense of smell. The simple truth is, to Ivan, canine outsiders have so little value they may as well be invisible. Unfortunately, this is not the case with a couple of his not quite so driven littermates, who are still in training but have a long way to go to reach indifference with other dogs. This is mostly due to their owner's inexperience in managing dogs of this intensity (I believe the dogs are more challenging than what their owners bargained for). As difficult as it is for these owners to hear, the quashing of their dog's aggressive behavior is a terribly pressing matter. It's not simply uncomfortable to deal with, but each hostile experience adds to a negative pattern. The longer this training pattern is allowed to stand, the more difficult it becomes to expunge.

Eighteen months of considerate direction has brought out the best in my companions. Both Hector and Ivan, although on slightly different training paths, have developed into confident, animated, and responsive teammates. I feel privileged to have had the opportunity to work with such fine animals. So, carefully choose the training approach that best suits your situation and your dog's personality. No matter how you decide to shape your dog's behavior, a direct Paddle Upstream route or an indirect Portage Overland approach, don't lose sight of your goal as training progresses. Self control over hostile behavior while in the immediate presence of canine competitors is the goal, and that's where we want our companions to end up.

Chapter Four

Predatory Aggression

Movement stimulates! That's just the way it is for certain dogs. A cat, a bird, or a cyclist can all represent the same kind of moving trigger for a predatory canine. There are a number of breeds that lean more heavily in that direction like representatives of the terrier, sporting, hound, and herding groups. If a person had a desire to rid their barn or ship of rodents, employing the skills of an energized rat terrier would be a sound plan. Should you have a penchant for freshly prepared grouse, owning a well bred Brittany would bring that delicacy much closer to the table. Nothing beats a good hound when assistance is needed in locating an elusive woodland creature like a raccoon or wild boar. Imagine trying to round up all of your pastured sheep without the help of a hard working Border collie. So, if a person needs some kind of animal captured, flushed, treed, or corralled there's no better friend to call on for aid than Canis familiaris.

I would be willing to bet that most of you reading this book don't have a rat problem and Thanksgiving turkey is about as wild a game bird as your palate desires. I suspect that most of my reading audience have never dreamed of running up on a bear held at bay or entertained the idea of owning a ranch. Even though most of you fall into this category of average pet owners, you may still live with a dog that exudes this kind of potential. Living with an unemployed dog that's bent towards work can be a real challenge. It doesn't matter how arduously you labor to convince your amped up Jack Russell to "disengage, we don't have a rat problem"; his probable reaction to those efforts will be, "Gotcha! I'll just move on to cats". Taking the hound out of the Treeing Walker isn't possible, no differently than trying to remove a facet from a princess cut diamond. If you change the cut, you change the diamond. Similarly, if you remove the retrieve drive from the Labrador, you don't have a duck dog.

Directing his energy and assertiveness to move the sheep

Much more so than people, dogs are honest and true to their nature; and the stronger the nature, the more inclined one is to be true in its expression. Now that brings us around to the topic of selective breeding, a process man has subjected dogs to for probably more than twenty-five thousand years. This process works. That's why we have the pleasure of sharing this planet with the multifarious forms of Canis familiaris. Even though essentially out of the same gene pool, it is difficult to view the Yorkshire terrier and the English Mastiff as the same species. Bottom line, if a person purchases a herding dog, at least some desire or drive to gather and move animals should be expected as part of this canine's nature. Selective breeding can also mean the closer a dog is bred to actual working lines, the more intense this desire or expression

Predatory Aggression

is likely to be. So, if you acquire a Brittany pup whose mother and father were both field trial champions, you can rest assured this puppy came out of the womb with a higher than average interest in birds. The act of acquiring a Border collie doesn't mean that in order to keep your little herder happy you have to get into the sheep business, it means if you didn't plan on ways to channel and direct this herding energy then you may be a little myopic and asking for trouble.

By reading this far, I'm sure you're picking up on a consistent theme: **"There's probably nothing wrong with your dog." He turned out the way he was supposed to.** He's neither diabolical nor saintly; he is simply a marvelous variation of canine potential that should not be allowed to control your team! Shaping a specific dog's behavior within the limitations of his unique possibilities is the path of a realistic, conscientious, and compassionate trainer. Remember, changing a dog's character is not really possible in a practical sense, and we're not going to alter his personality or crush his spirit either. In this chapter, I'm going to help you manage, but not change, the dog you have.

Single minded focus helps move the sheep

Roscoe is approaching two years old as I write this chapter. He is a robust Border collie mix who has passed through several homes. Today, he is living in downtown suburbia in a modest home with a small fenced in back yard. The ordinary family of four (two adults and two children) that care for Roscoe now have had him not quite a year, which is longer than any other owner, and they couldn't be more fond of him. However, barely over month after moving in with his new family, Roscoe killed one of their two cats. The family spent about a month trying to find a suitable home for him but they were unsuccessful. They even considered the proverbial farm where bad dogs are shipped off to but they remembered that's exactly where he came from due to his interest chicken killing and horse chasing. The farmer had received Roscoe from a couple that lived in a developed, but rural area, where he roamed unfenced. He became quite the deer and cyclist chaser. When Roscoe began catching cyclists, the couple decided he'd be better off on a farm. Painfully, the family came to the realization that no one would be willing to take responsibility for Roscoe with his well developed predatory behavior, so they decided to call me and see if it would be possible to fix their new friend.

My first impressions of Roscoe are representative of him today: happy, social, confident, and athletic. A person's initial response to the family's request may have been, "What is there to fix?" When I looked at Roscoe I saw a handsome, intelligent animal that was adroitly carrying out his natural duties of capturing prey. One might say, "Roscoe's business was subduing prey, and business was good!" Of course I did understand the family's predicament, so we discussed all the challenges that lie ahead if they wanted to pursue training. The entire family genuinely liked Roscoe, so they held nothing against him for killing one of their treasured house companions. This meant we could begin Roscoe's instruction with no emotional hurdles, which is a critical prerequisite in any dog training program dealing with hostile behavior.

My first job was convincing this family that although Roscoe's predatory drive is absolutely natural and necessary in the wild, it doesn't have to be acted upon in his current domestic situation. No differently than we teach our house pets to override their urge to urinate until the appropriate time and place is made available, we can teach a predatory dog to ignore his desire to chase until the appropriate time, place, and target is made available. Encouraging a dog to discriminate is the key to controlling predatory aggression. Exactly like we demonstrate to our canine companions what is okay to eat, we'll reveal to our predator what is okay to chase and subdue. For any animal, there is not a more basic instinctual need to be satisfied than when you're hungry and food is available. However, everyday hungry house pets are taught to leave the juicy roast on the table and wait for the dry, bland kibble. Discrimination is the name of the game. You can eat this, but you can't eat that," or "you can urinate here, but not in there," In Roscoe's case, "you can chase or capture this, but you must leave that alone."

Training makes the drive and aggression useful

There is little doubt, that if a driven dog is given an avenue of expression or an acceptable channel for his drive and energy, then the task of self control is more palatable. The plan with Roscoe was to shift his predatory focus from cats and cyclists to fast moving balls, flying discs, and tug-o-war ropes. At the same time we were building interest in the new forms of prey to subdue, we were also quashing interest in the old moving targets. Moving and subdue are key words here. A fast moving target is captivating to a predator with strong connections to his rudimentary hunting drives. This can often be witnessed at a zoo while observing the reaction of some large cats as children go racing past their enclosure. Besides the thrill of exertion, part of the exhilaration that comes from the chase is the anticipated capture. Capture of course means a chance to use those impressive teeth and powerful jaws to crush and shake the life out of something. I will admit, even at fifty-four years old, I still get the biggest kick out of watching a dog shake the "entrails" out of a stuffed toy or rope. That act is so engrossing and so satisfying to even the smallest and most innocuous of canines, it's impossible not to be amused by such a spectacle.

Choosing the right time and place to build interest in new targets is a critical consideration when working with a predatory dog like Roscoe. I wanted to make sure when I brought out a ball or tug-o-war rope that there was nothing more enticing in the training area that would redirect Roscoe's attention. There is not a toy made that's going to hold a candle to a living animal for an experienced predator. Roscoe's new prey development began in one of my large training rooms where I knew there would be no interference from birds or joggers. I purposely set up his first session bright and early one morning so he would be bubbling with energy, fully evacuated and hungry. In this state of being, Roscoe was truly chomping at the bit for stimulation. A perfect start to the day, if left up to him, would have been routing out the house cat or running down a cyclist. Since these options weren't available, racing me to catch the elusive bouncing ball or jumping after the swinging rope for grab and growl was the best game in town.

In order to heighten Roscoe's interest in the new targets and the game itself, I kept our training sessions short, always ending the exercises before he was fully satisfied or exhausted. By concluding each training experience this way, Roscoe was left wanting and looking forward to the next opportunity of chase and capture. Because of his family's strong commitment to training, and their willingness to leave Roscoe with me throughout the week, I was afforded a few instruction opportunities with him each day. Every training morning opened with the prey building exercises and every evening closed with a repeat. The central portion of the day was devoted to the pivotal work of distraction desensitization. Having covered the details of this conditioning process in chapter two, I will only outline the particulars of a predator and prey situation in this section. The simple truth is, although the drives and the targets may vary, the steps of self control development around distractions in any given case are relatively uniform. Aggression intensity, strength of drive and energy level are the important variables in a training equation. These variables should always be honestly assessed (in terms of high, medium or low) before instruction officially begins. Once you feel comfortable having evaluated your canine student, guide your overly zealous predator through his prey distraction desensitization with the same consideration used to walk a dog aggressive canine through his dog distraction conditioning.

In Roscoe's case, the central part of training day one involved a trip out to the Black Walnut trees behind our training center. That's where the squirrels live. On any given day of the year, they are busy taking care of squirrel business, boldly hopping along the ground, jumping from tree to tree, or simply lounging on our fence. Their neighborhood is the training center's outside instruction area. Dogs are part of their life and they appear to get a genuine kick out of taunting the new canine students. The squirrels do their distraction job so well I would gladly pay them for their services. With the first step out the back door, my eyes are fixed on Roscoe since we're headed straight for squirrel country. Even though this fellow has never been in our back yard and is completely unaware of the critters that lie ahead, he is on full alert. Just like a dog-on-dog aggression case, Roscoe is searching for targets nearly all the time. In order to get the jump on his aggressive explosion, I need to begin our walk far away from any prey animals. This allows me the opportunity to witness the spark of predatory hostility and seize the moment with a leash and collar correction while his energy and commitment are at low levels. Keen supervision and fast action on my part mean I won't have to fight as hard to quash Roscoe's interest in the squirrels. As I described in chapter two, the instant I bring Roscoe's attention around to me, I'll engage him with some positive communication and a light directive. With this approach, a negative experience is quickly turned into a positive.

Since Roscoe was a very experienced and determined predator (approaching Hector in challenge), I chose a direct training route for his prey desensitization. So, with Roscoe comfortably on my general left at the end of a loose six foot leash (the walking exercise in Ten Natural Steps to Training the Family Dog), we proceeded towards the prey. Remember, my eyes were locked on the canine student from the first step out the door to ensure that I would not be caught off guard. Any time I'm working with a new dog, even in simple formal command instruction, I visually focus on the dog-in-training and monitor everything else peripherally. The distance from building to walnut trees is about thirty yards. In the first half of this interval, I made a point to praise Roscoe for pleasant walking and I stopped frequently to pet him. Knowing in a matter of yards we were going to be in a trouble zone, I wanted to establish early on that we were a good team and the entire world was in peaceful balance. A full fifteen yards before the actual tree line, Roscoe caught sight of a bushy tailed rodent and his head lowered, his tail raised, his pace quickened, and his brain forgot all about me! All these changes in my attentive, light hearted student occurred in the briefest of moments. He had instantly transformed into a predatory machine and squirrel was on the menu. Our happy team work, the tranquil world, and his all important pack leader lost all value when prey came into sight. I was looking for this moment, and the real purpose for our walk was to arrange for this exact morphing opportunity. Since Roscoe had turned into a squirrel seeking missile, he missed my, one hundred and eighty degree change in direction. As he sped up heading due south toward squirrel country, I quickened my pace (after the stealthy direction change) heading due north back to the building. I used no commands or signals of any kind during the direction change.

The entire idea here is to drive home the point, "Roscoe, when you shift focus to prey, you pull focus from the primary handler and that has consequences." The deterrent for squirrel chasing in this instance was the abrupt reverse in direction Roscoe experienced when he ran out of leash. My intention was to jar my student's focus free from the prey in the south and bring it immediately to his handler in the north. Given our weight differences, even though my student was fully committed to seize his quarry, he had no alternative other than to spin around and head north once he'd reached leashes end. With the simultaneous goal of efficacy and safety, I utilized a twenty-two inch long, three millimeter, slip chain collar and a six foot long, heavy weight, leather leash. This gear provided comfort, safety, and fast action, which Roscoe and I needed to get off of squirrels and on with our pleasant walk.

Make sure you have enough longline to stop a fast charging dog after squirrels

Thwarting Roscoe's chase and capture attempt once was definitely not a life changing event for him. After all, he was a seasoned predator and had successfully gotten around obstacles in the past to pursue his passion. He wasn't about to throw in the towel simply because I had spun him around one time. So the moment Roscoe settled into an attentive, loose leash walk, I turned once again for squirrel country. On the second attempt, I ran into essentially a repeat of our first approach at almost exactly the same distance from the prey. This wasn't a surprise given my student's experience and passion for his work. By approach number four however, Roscoe's bolt for the rodents became more like a creep forward. We were able to walk much closer to the trees before he started to move ahead. Finally, on the seventh approach, I was able to walk Roscoe on a loose leash, at my general left, all the way through squirrel country and back without a single break away. Keep in mind that up to the seventh attempt, I was maneuvering back and forth between the walnut trees and the training center building. I was careful not to deviate from my original plan of walking peacefully from point "A" to point "B". I did not alter my pace, trajectory, or mood during the first six attempts at approaching the squirrels. **I can't stress enough how important it is for the management of aggression to consistently demonstrate that the team leader is steadfast when it comes to plans and protocol.** If a confident canine student detects his primary handler acquiescing under pressure or witnesses the handler's obvious avoidance of conflict over policy, then the stage has been set for a challenge over team leadership! That's why I set up the simplest of exercises when I began Roscoe's instruction. He was tough, strong, and determined, so I had to be sure what I set out to do with him I could finish. I not only wanted to complete our simple task of walking peacefully into squirrel country, but I also wanted to conduct the instruction in an upbeat style. A positive mindset is the mode for clear thought, understanding and retention. No matter how challenging the dog, I never want my canine students to dread handling or instruction. When dread takes over a dog's mind, thoughts of escape fill his brain rather than thoughts of accomplishment. Please heed this advice and work very hard not to bite off more than you can chew. **Structure your dog's training so that the mission is accomplished in small steps.** Think of carving a statue as an analogy to dog training. A sculptor is careful not to take off too large a piece of stone with his chisel strike. In fact, the closer he gets to the finished work the more careful he becomes so he doesn't ruin the entire work of art for the sake of a little time.

Roscoe required several training sessions over a couple of days to be able to walk straight out of the building and up to the squirrels without incident. Just as soon as he was comfortable with this new self control responsibility, I set up a cyclist scenario as our next task. Although this was more challenging than the squirrel walk, I thought it was a manageable step for my quick study. When you are guiding a dog through a training process, try not to delay in setting up new challenges. Think of momentum as a spring board which helps launch the canine student up to the next level of responsiveness and control.

For helpers, I almost always recruit one of my trusted, dog savvy coworkers who know how to think on the fly. This helps to ensure safety for all concerned, including the dog, in the event some part of the training process goes awry. Practically every new training challenge is more productive when set up under controlled conditions. Having controls or parameters in place is exponentially more important when a trainer is working with an aggressive dog. Our goal always is to capitalize on success and momentum, but caution should guide a trainer when moving into real world situations. When working with a hostile canine, I double up on the controlled training tests (which are usually more challenging than true world experiences) to ensure that only minimal effort will be needed to get a dog to reliably respond under real life conditions. Remember to cautiously enter the everyday world, but don't avoid it. Too much delay or trepidation will only eat away at your hard earned and evanescent momentum. With dogs like Roscoe and Hector, I seize every advantage available because they always add up!

Days after schooling began for Roscoe, I was ready to add the new cyclist exercise. Even though I continually added to my student's plate, I opened and closed each training day with chase and capture games (using "prey" of my choice, e.g. ball, disc, and rope). The first cyclist Roscoe was exposed to since his instruction began with me was Josh, my youngest and most recent addition to the training staff, who is always game to be bait. Before walking Roscoe out front, I had Josh pedal his bike down the road about fifty yards, and wait for my signal to come riding by. As far as my canine student was concerned, the two of us were simply walking out to the mailbox, which happened to be alongside the same rode that cyclist (his favorite prey, Roscoe might add) sometimes used. How serendipitous!

Be quick with your step and use both feet if you have to

Just as I stepped out the front door of the training center, I gave a big wave to Josh to start peddling our way. Synchronizing the bicycle ride with our mailbox approach was critical in order to arrange the optimal distance for dog stimulation, rider safety, and handler action, all in the same moment. Again for the purpose of effectiveness, I had Roscoe wearing a three millimeter width slip collar, and I had a heavy, six foot long, leather leash firmly in grip. Just like the first squirrel walk, as Roscoe and I headed across the parking lot towards the mailbox, I insisted on a loose leash and casual pace. I wanted no indication for Roscoe that any special event was on the horizon. **With any set up or controlled training exercise, I go to great pains to bring about a real life feel.** A successful trainer will always work as diligently as possible to prevent a canine student from catching wind of an arranged learning experience. The last thing any handler wants to create in their dog's mind is ring or training awareness. With a training aware student or a ring wise (as it's known in animal competition circles) dog, two separate rule systems are developed simultaneously. One set of rules exists for the dog when it's training time, and an entirely different set apply to real world conditions. This type of awareness develops when a canine student notices distinct and consistent differences in the handler's behavior, equipment usage, or phoniness in distraction interaction during training experiences as compared to the more normal experiences of everyday life. Safe guards against such awareness development are: continuity in the use and wearing of handling gear (collars, leashes, long lines, etc.) before, during and after training sessions, normal and consistent handler mannerisms and communication before, during and after each training experience, and any 'helpers" recruited to assist in the training process must role play accurately. Assistants should step into their character before exposure to the dog, and it is important to maintain that facade until completely out of the dog's sight and the training environment. Careful attention given to these safeguards assures a smooth transition from training scenarios to real world situations.

Roscoe caught sight of the cyclist before we were anywhere near the mailbox. That wasn't a negative at all, and his early notice actually gave me more operating room to work in my parking lot rather than in the street. Even though I had spent the last several days conditioning Roscoe to have self control around squirrels, he shot off like a rocket when he zeroed in on Josh. In this situation I didn't need the stealthy right about turn to expose my predatory student's misdirected focus. All I had to do was stand fast and prepare for Roscoe's seventy-five pounds to abruptly run out of leash. By the time his own force had spun him around, I was turned and walking back to the building. Judging by the expression on his face, Roscoe seemed somewhat stunned and a little disappointed to find himself also walking back to the training center rather than in hot pursuit of his prey.

In this exercise, like the squirrel walk, I used no verbal warnings to prepare my student for the negative consequence that would be connected to his negative behavior. There are a number of reasons for this quiet approach to leash action. First, by warning a dog before a leash and collar action, a handler allows the student to mentally prepare for the correction, which in turn lessens its effect. Second, if a warning always precedes a corrective action, most dogs will learn to take advantage of this delay in the delivery of the true negative consequence and continue with the unwanted behavior for a moment longer, while his handler's negative utterances float off with the breeze. Third, a warning is an additional unnecessary, step in a two step process (negative behavior is connected to a meaningful, negative consequence).

Here are some guiding thoughts to go along with these reasons for quiet correction. Think of the average dog as being a very physical animal, much more so than people. This means that actual physical experience (both positive and negative) is going to have more impact on your canine companion than any words that come out of your mouth. Streamline your dog's thought processes as much as possible by keeping the connection between his actions and the resulting consequences clear and obstruction free. The muddier the water is with handler emotion, threats, and directives, the more difficult it becomes for a dog to glean any meaningful information from an experience.

This last thought is one of the reasons why I don't utilize formal commands when I'm trying to eliminate a negative behavior in a canine student. For example, if I would have commanded Roscoe to come the moment he bolted after the cyclist and he refused because he was in the heat of the chase, I would immediately follow up with a meaningful correction. Now, in his mind there's probably little doubt that he received the negative consequence for failing to respond to the all important command that just preceded the correction, having little to do with chasing cyclists. On the other hand, let's say Roscoe did respond to my command to come. In order to maintain consistency in training and reinforce the importance of following commands, I should follow his response with some kind of reward. So with this outcome like the first, I'm not addressing the cyclist issue. I'm only putting this predatory problem off to another day, when I may have my back turned to the road while I'm mulching around a tree. In this scenario, unfortunately for a passing cyclist, I won't be quick enough on the draw to command Roscoe to come before he meets the bike rider. Facilitate your canine student's information gathering by omitting warnings and leaving out commands. By doing so a dog is left with the cleanest possible lesson; undesirable hostility is connected to an unpleasant consequence and conversely, control of hostility is connected to a pleasant consequence. Allow your dog to choose his course of action (the primary handler will supply the appropriate consequence) and self-educate through this heuristic method.

What follows is a personal experience and a natural example of the canine heuristic (trial and error) learning method. About two years ago, my daughter Heidi came to live with me while she and her husband transitioned out of the Navy and back home. Along with Heidi came her loyal companion K2, a fifteen year old, deaf, Norwegian elkhound. The very first evening of Heidi's stay, we were on the front porch drinking tea and catching up, when K2 decided to venture from the porch. Unbeknownst to him, K2 was following his nose along my trail that led straight to an active beehive. This was a brand new colony of bees, so I had to feed them regularly (hence the path). In K2's mind he had found a happening trail that must lead to an exciting place.

For those of you who have never been around domestic bees, you might be surprised to learn what gentle and forgiving creatures they are. I could stand a complete stranger immediately in front of the hive opening and the little buzzers will fly between the legs, under the arms, or over the shoulders to make way inside their house, but they wouldn't think of stinging anyone for this inconvenience. Now if a stranger pokes around the physical opening or raises the hive lid, he may be in for a little stinging action. Remember, K2 can't hear a thing (he responds well to hand signals when his failing vision is locked on a handler). As he closes in on the hive, Heidi rises from her chair to retrieve him. Well aware that Heidi and her companion were going to be living with me for months and envisioning having to retrieve this little fellow every day at some point, I came up with some wise fatherly advice. I suggested we finish our tea and see what happens!

Knowing that my colony of domestic, honey bees were not of the African killer type, I wasn't too worried about K2's health. Watching from the porch, Heidi and I could almost hear K2's thoughts as he approached the hive: "What in the world is this! And what is Matthew doing out here so often? I smell propolis, honey, and sugar water. It seems like the odor comes from this little hole where all the buzzing flies are coming in and out. Maybe I should get little closer to that hole. What in the world! These aren't flies, they bite and this box is full of them!" As K2 is high tailing it back to the porch while shaking his head, we could see his final thoughts about beehives written all over his face: "Whatever treasure may lie in that box, Matthew and the biting flies can keep it. From now on, I'll watch that happening place from a safe distance." And he did! Heidi and K2 lived with me for about ten months. Every other day when I fed my colony of hard workers, K2 studied intently from about twelve feet away. He allowed the bees to thrive and be happy; they in turn caused him no grief. This was a priceless example of natural learning without the help or interference of human beings. I just recounted for you a life lesson that wasn't terribly emotional or personal. It was simply educational; a heuristic experience for a quick canine study that can serve as a good dog training model (without the bee stings of course!).

Roscoe made rapid progress in cyclist control in only a couple of training sessions. There were a few reasons for his success. First of all, he really was a bright fellow and connected the dots very easily. Secondly, he had barely finished his squirrel lesson when I began the cyclist training and I'm sure to Roscoe they felt quite similar. Lastly, unlike the squirrels that I had no control over, I could arrange for Josh and other helpers to make pass after pass on bikes, thereby accumulating numerous learning experiences for Roscoe every training session. The goal of this exercise was to walk to the mailbox and down the street with Roscoe beside me on a loose draped six foot leash, as my various helpers flew past on bikes at close proximity. I also wanted to cross the road in front or behind a moving cyclist and call the rider over to shake my hand without Roscoe losing composure.

Achieving a dependable loose leash walk to the mailbox and down the road only took about four training sessions over a two day instruction period. It took another day for my student to gain true composure with an approaching cyclist and tolerate a follow up hand shake. All in all, this six foot leash portion of Roscoe's training rolled along smoothly. He required strong leash and collar action mostly to counter his speed and body weight during a pursuit, but not because of belligerence. Given Roscoe's history, I had mentally prepared (prior to the start of his training) to revisit training scenarios many times in order to quash his long standing habits but he demonstrated early on that wasn't going to be necessary. Once Roscoe showed that he was on board, he didn't slip back much. He was born a team player. All I did was convince him that he wasn't the team leader!

With an experienced predatory dog that's proven to be fast as lightning, long line work is a must in achieving long term training success. By utilizing a one inch wide, ten meter long, nylon line I was able demonstrate to Roscoe that even though I was a substantial distance away, the outcome of chasing squirrels or a cyclist was going to be exactly the same as it was when we were close together. I definitely needed to be careful working strong, fast Roscoe on such a long line. If he caught me off guard and built up twenty feet of running steam before I secured the line, there's little doubt that I'd end up with two blistered hands. The same could be said of my legs if Roscoe bolted off after a neighbor's cat while I was busy watering the trees with the long line wrapped around my ankles. In order to solidify his training, it was imperative that I convey a natural environment when the two of us were outside. The long line allowed me to do that, but I had to be aware of the line without calling Roscoe's attention to it. As before, I must put real effort in creating a long line scenario set up so that my student wouldn't suspect the unfolding events were actually training traps. The plan was for me to appear busy (but watchful), while Roscoe was encouraged to hang out.

Hanging out is a very important condition for an aggressive dog during self control training. A canine student must be afforded the opportunity for autonomous actions (within common sense parameters like restricted area and limited time frame) in order to develop habitually good decision making. For hostility control especially, I shy away from a training strategy that pits a target's magnetism against a formal command's adhesiveness. Dependable off leash control around squirrels, cyclists, and cats is what Roscoe's family needed in order to keep him. To have any chance of reaching this high bar, Roscoe had to feel a similar kind of equipment freedom and naturalness during his instruction that he did outside of training. Along with this off leash atmosphere, I had to arrange an instruction environment that gave me the necessary advantage to thwart any attempt Roscoe made at chasing the wrong kind of prey. The ten meter long line helped me on both of these fronts.

I put a long line on Roscoe while we were still in the house, about thirty minutes before going outside. This early preparation helped make the line disappear. The more time Roscoe spent dragging around the extended leash and out of hand, the less significant it became. This desensitizing process works with any type of training equipment. With the long line securely in place and well out of mind (as far as Roscoe was concerned), my newly reformed predator and I headed out the back door for squirrel country. After I opened the door, I gave Roscoe the go ahead while I held the door open allowing all the line to pass through. I purposely avoided picking it up or carrying it, because I wanted no attention directed that way. Now, out in the back yard Roscoe was free to wander about dragging around the (by now) insignificant line. He actually wore it as easily as he did his own tail. In fact, that's a good way for a handler to view the long line, it's just like the dog-in-training is dragging around an extra long tail that can be very convenient to grab from time to time.

While Roscoe was sniffing around and generally hanging out, I made a point to walk over and talk to Kathy (one of my long time associates) who happened to be working a little Scottish terrier in the vicinity of the squirrels. With a couple of busy acres at his disposal, it was easy for Roscoe to get lost in smells or become distracted by clients working outside with their dogs. Whenever he drifted further than about twenty-five feet from me, I would quietly make my way towards his line, pick it up, and give a reasonable tug to snag his attention. The sharpness of the tug depends entirely on the specific dog (hardness and determination considered) and the unique situation (egregious wrong doing or simply daydreaming into forgetfulness) you may find him in. With Roscoe's innocent wandering or absent mindedness (I considered these behaviors innocent because he was so new to training responsibilities) the look on his face after my tug was, "You rang?" His follow up behavior to an effective tug reflected a mindset of, "Wow! How'd we drift so far apart? I really got lost in my own plan didn't I? I need to check in more often."

Roscoe's freedom lies within two parameters: number one, proximity to the handler (within twenty-five feet, and no help from commands or restraints) and number two, don't bother anybody (man or beast) in any way. I wanted to make sure Roscoe was clear on this before he was faced with a real challenge. So there was no rush to move into squirrel country, but that's where Kathy and I were slowly headed. Before we actually arrived at the walnut trees, Kathy's new student was building up steam. Whiffs of familiar quarry sent the feisty Scotty into a whining frenzy. The little dog cast her head about so high that her short, front legs weren't even touching the ground. The Scotty's excited behavior had the same effect on Roscoe as if sounding an alarm, "Squirrels on the loose!"

For Roscoe, the newly discovered long line freedom that was now coupled with a potent atmosphere of competition (generated by the Scotty's presence), made the call to arms more than he could resist. Like a black and white bolt, Roscoe blew past me and Kathy fully determined that no short legged Scotty would ever beat him out of a potential squirrel dinner. Fortunately for me and the greater good of training, as Roscoe raced past his long, blue, nylon tail trailed conveniently behind. Without command or warning, I jumped on the long line with both feet. My one hundred and eighty pounds was just enough to bring Roscoe to an abrupt stop, but not enough to turn his full attention around to me. Accordingly, not allowing for an extra moment to think about squirrels, I picked up the long line with two hands and jolted the trainee's focus back to me. I delivered a considerably stronger jolt here, because in this learning situation Roscoe's behavior was not quite as innocent as it was in the absent minded drifting. After this experience, the expression on Roscoe's face reflected the stronger impression I was hoping to make, "I'm really sorry! I'm going to do better," and he did!

While Kathy had her hands full of Scotty on their first day of predatory training, Roscoe never gave me any further trouble over squirrels. At this stage of training I introduced a little stimulation with tug-o-war and chasing the flying disc all within proximity of squirrel activity. Although it was his first play session next to the one time quarry, he kept reasonable focus on our games and genuinely seemed to enjoy the experience even though it didn't involve squirrels. A handler of a predatory dog should always keep in mind when your canine student's energy level raises so does the likelihood he'll break for quarry. This meant energizing Roscoe around the walnut trees was putting him to a real test. Proving to me that he could play with relative ease and wander around squirrel country without drifting too far or bothering anyone meant the next training session would allow for a more challenging training environment. Out front, Roscoe would be free to watch a cyclist pedal by as he roamed about within the two main parameters we already established.

Just as I did with the squirrel sessions, I connected the long line to Roscoe's working collar inside the training center about thirty minutes before heading out front. Whenever possible, it's best to have training equipment and the helpers in place and out of the dog's mind well before the instruction session begins. For this episode of cyclist control, I had a female rider launch from further down the road so that she could reach high speed by the time she passed the training center. I calculated our approach to the street so that as the cyclist pedaled by, Roscoe would still be a full long line length from the road itself. This gave us plenty of operating room so if Roscoe bolted after the fast moving target, I would have time to react with the long line and negate his charge, keeping both rider and dog safe from harm. Often in a high risk (of injury or failure) training situation like this one, where I'm working with a dog on a free ranging long line, I keep one of my hands through the handle of the line to act as a safety net in order to prevent loose dog mishaps. When I wear a long line like this, I'm very careful to act naturally disengaged from the dog while appearing busy. That means I use both hands while washing the car and spying on my student. If a quick canine study observes his handler standing like a statue with an awkwardly extended arm, you can rest assured he'll smell a trap.

With the rider's first pass, Roscoe flinched but did not break for the prey. He nearly gave himself whiplash though, checking to see if I was watching him or really washing the car. Since Roscoe held so well without command or restraint, I made the effort to walk over and pet him up. By the time I got back to my pseudo duties, the cyclist had returned faster and at a closer distance. She also added a little squeal, which added some realism and just enough stimulation to entice Roscoe into a half charge. His truncated pursuit presented an excellent opportunity to further develop roadside etiquette. I wanted to convey to him that any commitment to chasing bike riders, even half hearted, ends with a negative consequence (a substantial jolt). Of note, by the time Roscoe made this charge, he already had enough instruction to consider even a small commitment to the wrong kind of prey a breach in our training agreement. That meant I did not consider his inappropriate, predatory action to be innocent. Therefore, in order to fully extinguish that unwanted behavior, I had to deliver a stronger negative consequence with each repeated offense (large or small). It really didn't matter how I got the job done using the long line (a stronger single jolt or rapid fire, multiple jolts), Roscoe needed to feel an increase in deterrent strength. Through association, my canine student understood that repeated infractions were bringing on a rise in correction intensity. In other words, the game he loved was becoming increasingly more negative and barely worth pursuing (we were at the threshold of unwanted behavior extinction).

By her third and fourth passes, the pedaling prey could not attract anything but a brief glance from my student. In fact, he was quite content to hang out close to me while I finished up my duties. This turn towards self control gave me every reason to dote over Roscoe for his incredibly good behavior! Varying the training set up (utilizing multiple riders, walking Roscoe down the road as cyclist passed and playing ball with Roscoe in full view of the riders) over the following few days, only tempted my predator slightly. As he did with squirrel conditioning, when it came to cyclist control Roscoe demonstrated he wasn't just bright; he was also a team player, and he wanted to work with me, not against me (not all dogs are man's best friend and feel this way). Through two full weeks of basic obedience training along with his predatory drive control, Roscoe never lost his happy tail or his enthusiasm for life. Inside of a month, he had smoothly and naturally shifted most of his predatory passion over to the appropriate targets we introduced on his first day of instruction.

I want to leave you with some closing thoughts. Real life situations should be the training atmosphere for a canine student because real life control is the ultimate goal. This is especially important when curbing predatory aggression. The dog-in-training should view the handler's prearranged opportunity to pursue and capture prey as genuine. Each time his attempt to chase and seize a particular target is thwarted, a little bit of his confidence and enthusiasm for the sport is lost. Eventually with enough failed experiences in succession, the predator will lose enough interest in the targeted prey to cease his attempts to chase and capture. **I don't want the reader to forget that the exhilaration of the pursuit is of itself rewarding, and to the dog it is worth repeating even though there was no prize at the end. So preventing the chase is just as important to training success as preventing the capture.**

From the outset of training, I selected squirrels as the first prey to work around because they were stimulating to Roscoe but not quite as attractive as cyclists. The squirrel scenario was also a very manageable situation for me to set up and control as compared to working with cats or chickens. The cyclist challenge represented a step up in both intensity and management, yet it remained within the scope of what I could set up as a successful learning experience. I also chose these two forms of prey because they are fair representations of predatory targets as a whole. With predatory aggression, the self control that results from training around one type of target carries over to subsequent learning situations involving different prey. So what we accomplish in area "A" we utilize to reach our goal in area "B". Manage your predatory dog's instruction accordingly.

Another training element that assisted to Roscoe's successful development of self control was the intentional transfer of his natural predatory drive to acceptable prey. As you recall, from the earliest moments of training Roscoe received regular and stimulating exercise with bouncing balls, flying discs, and tug-o-war ropes. These acceptable targets gave Roscoe a positive and much needed outlet for his creator given potential. Although transferring predatory drive from undesirable to desirable targets is not a prerequisite for training success, I've found it does give a driven dog an opportunity for some stimulation and satisfaction, which in turn leads to a happier student that is more open to suggestion. Besides, chasing after things is good exercise and a real health benefit.

Chapter Five
Defensive Aggression

Whether a watch dog, body guard, security patrol, or just an alarm, most dog fanciers admire the effectiveness of Canis familiaris in all of these roles. Casually surveying the three to four hundred civilian clients I see a year, I can pass on to you that a large percentage of dog owners purchased their companion specifically for this type of service. When a canine companion jumps to meet danger ahead of all others within his pack, or when the family pet sounds the alarm over impending peril in the wee hours of the morning, most of us would consider these traits admirable. However, canine defensive and territorial potential needs to be handled as a double edged sword, especially when considering extreme canine personalities. If a cherished watch dog launches into action against a friend rather than a foe, that admirable behavior instantly becomes abominable. The very same hostile behavior is either considered admirable or abominable based on the target it was directed towards. A body guard that can't be civil in his behavior when needed is no longer an asset but a liability to his family.

In this section of the book, I'm going to examine the specifics of a defensive canine personality and then transition into the true territorial type of aggressive potential. Even though these two forms of hostile expression appear similar on the surface, a family dog can be bent clearly more one way than the other. In fact, we regularly work with each type of aggressive personality that is primarily concerned with the triggers associated with threat upon territory or threat upon self, but not both! With a defensive dog, threat or call to duty is all about proximity, and in the case of a territorial canine it's all about perimeter. What is really important about the distinction between a defensive and a territorial dog are the triggers the handler needs to vigilantly monitor. Our training approach and problem solving strategy will also differ between these two types of hostility. Categorizing aggressive behavior in this book or at the training center outlines (for a trainer) the parameters a dog needs to work within. The labels I use at the training center, or in this handling guide, are for the purpose of understanding the dog in training as best we can, so we can set up the proper training environment that will bring about the very best results.

Defensive aggression kicks in when a stranger approaches

Tendencies towards aggressive behaviors can often be recognized in the very young pup. I routinely conduct temperament assessments on young dogs and evaluate entire litters of pups for placement. My charge is to identify character traits and project into the future how they will express themselves at full maturity. Recently I sat across from a reserved, ten week old Lhasa apso that steadily growled while she stared at me from between her owner's feet. The first thought that ran through my mind was "This pup is awfully young to be so serious!" If at this innocent, dependent age a pup is heavily concerned over the presence of an outsider and already separates "us" from "them", I know I'm looking at a formidable defensive dog in the making. This young Lhasa I'm referring to is playful and cuddly with family members. She's even wiggly and highly sociable with other non-threatening dogs. Only when she perceives a threat (monster) does she throw up defensive signals. Monsters to her are strange, potentially harmful entities both animate (an adult human visitor) and inanimate (a curb side garbage can). The Lhasa's owners don't encourage this kind behavior but they've watched it intensify despite their best efforts to quash it. Furthermore, they were appropriately concerned enough to bring her in for an evaluation early in life.

Many families seem almost shocked and relieved when I tell them that this kind of response in a young pup is not all that uncommon (especially within certain breed types), and inadequate socialization is probably not the sole cause for this visceral reaction to strangers. Just like this female Lhasa, most defensive dogs are born into this world, not created by it. Even though only ten weeks old, this little watch dog peers out through defensive glasses which unfortunately cannot be removed by any training effort. What we can do is teach her to override the natural, aggressive response to a villain in favor of the handler's suggestion of tolerance. Essentially, I've outlined the essence of defensive dog management with these two concepts: first, accept that we cannot alter how the defensive dog views the world and its inhabitants; second, focus on building acceptance of strangers and not fondness of them. If fondness follows acceptance during the instruction process then all the better, but our initial training goal needs to be realistic so that the canine student and handler don't succumb to frustration.

Being the perpetual owner of defensive dogs, I can assure you that tolerance of outsiders is enough. Your canine companion does not have to be best friends with your extended family in order to have them over for Thanksgiving. Pleasant social gatherings occur at my house on a regular basis even though my dogs don't necessarily like all of my guests. Keep in mind, it's not really about what your dog wants as much as it is about what you want! Never lose sight of your position as the team leader. Since it's your house, your policies matter most. I'm not satisfied unless my guests and my dog are comfortable, and only on rare occasions does that mean I put my companion in a safe place away from my company. As I outlined in Dog on Dog aggression, my responsibility as a primary handler is to protect innocent parties from being bothered or harmed by my companion. I am also responsible for protecting my canine friend from being bothered or harmed by others. If a defensive canine student has received sufficient training and the visitors within the home are well mannered, there is really no need to remove the watch dog from the family function. On the other hand, if you detect significant discomfort experienced by either a guest or your pet because of the proximity of one to the other, then removing the dog from the social setting would be in the best interest for all concerned.

Shaping defensiveness into personal protection

Resisting the urge to force friendship on a defensive canine companion seems almost impossible for some dog owners. Although well intentioned, this effort can all too often exacerbate the existing unease between a devoted canine and a visiting friend. The popular term "fear biter" can be a culprit in misleading dog owners who are trying to manage a hostile situation involving their defensive canine and a guest. This term leads an owner down the wrong path of alleviating fear by proving the visitor is friendly, not frightening. **Trying to improve a visitor's image through forced contact, face-to-face sweet talk, and offerings of favorite treats from a dirty hand (figuratively speaking of course), only serves to increase the negative vibrations.** Always perplexed over this futility in effort, defensive dog owners ask me on a regular basis, "Why is my dog still hostile towards guests?" I have found in most cases, the defensive dogs are not so much afraid of outsiders as they are irritated by them. Don't get me wrong, we also have our fair share of truly frightened canine students to deal with, but the outcome of forcing friendship on these personality types is about as dismal. The bottom line with most defensive family dogs is they're not particularly comfortable with many outsiders.

Not too long ago I watched a moving and enlightening video about a young autistic woman who had recently learned to communicate by manipulating a keyboard and computer. The insights she provided about the autistic mind were fascinating as well as invaluable to the medical field. One touching scene really stuck with me. The young woman's father asked why she would only rarely look at him over the years even though he continually encouraged her to do so. Her response brought him to tears. She said although she loved him very much, looking at his face was so frightening and painful she could only bring herself to do it once in a while. She explained that when she looked at a human face she saw a thousand pairs of eyes looking back at her. Essentially she saw a thousand-faced monster when she looked at her parents, and she learned to cope with that reality by avoiding face-to-face interaction. Sadly, no matter how much her parents loved her, no matter how well they cared for their daughter; they would always look like monsters to her. I can't help but think of this touching story when I deal with defensive and fearful dogs. If only they could talk, maybe they would say "I know you like Uncle Charlie, but no matter how hard you try all I'll see is a repulsive, frightening, or threatening monster!"

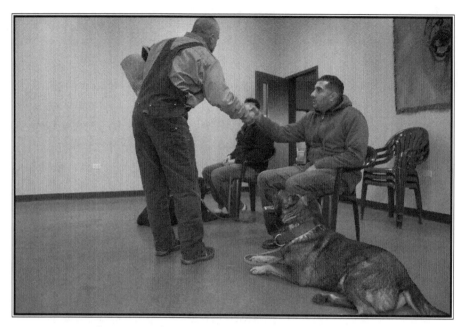

Personal protection dogs practicing self restraint after a confrontation.

Coping and tolerance are essential elements of defensive dog management. I'm going to tell you a story of my sister's gift for her daughter's birthday. One day at the training center I received a call from my sister, Jean. She had a simple question for her dog-training brother: "What do you think about miniature Dachshunds?" A fair enough question I thought, so I gave her a straight-forward, honest answer. I think they're as cute as stuffed animals, as animated as cartoons, as feisty as ferrets, and they usually come in one of two temperaments. They are either fearless or fearful and almost always very devoted to family (insiders), but unsure about outsiders. Even though they're not the best choice for a busy, young family, I like working with them. Jean was quiet for a moment after my response, and then she asked if I thought her family was too young and busy to manage one properly. I didn't think for a fraction of a moment, I said absolutely too much dog (albeit a small package) for your current social and "on the go" lifestyle. Another moment of silence followed before she said that she wanted to get one for Rachel's (my niece) birthday because they both thought they were cute. Without pause, I asked how many cute Dachshunds she had handled.

Her response of "none" was no surprise. I did reiterate, I think most miniature Dachshunds are as cute as they are a handful. I also mentioned again about the fearless or fearful characters they usually possess, and may translate into defensive or territorial behaviors. Jean then informed me that she already purchased an eight week old miniature Dachshund and her name was Rooney. I was quiet for a long moment, and then I mentioned how lucky she was to have a brother who could offer real insight into choosing a family dog. We were both quiet after my diatribe, and then I asked, "Is she cute?" That question opened the flood gates and Jean raved about Rooney's sweet personality and how quietly she studied everything. When I asked what Rooney's parents were like, my sister told me the breeder had to put away the puppies' mother so they could look at the litter, and she said the sire of the pups wasn't on the property because someone else owned him. Of course we planned for Rooney's basic training to begin at the first opportunity just in case some of my past experiences with Dachshund behaviors might come true. Jean and Rachel were so pleased with the new addition to the family that I didn't have the heart to further rain on their parade or mention a few red flags that came up in our conversation.

The feisty dog in a busy family scenario aside, I was a little concerned over Jean's comment about Rooney quietly studying everything. I wondered if what she saw was actually serious concern or worry over environmental changes and outsiders. I wish Jean would have said their new eight week old friend was bouncing around getting into everything and jumping on everyone. Even though these behaviors seem offensive, they're very easy to correct with training, and they are a sure sign that a newly weaned pup possesses a happy, healthy, and gregarious character. Since character or personality is not malleable like behavior and habits, it's much more important to be pleased with personality than behavior when selecting a pup. I also didn't like the fact that Rooney's mother had to be put away just so visitors could be around the pups. Even though a mother's protectiveness is understandable, was it extreme? Maybe the dam was highly defensive or territorial, which would have nothing to do with the pups. It's possible that Rooney's mother was simply happy, wild, or unruly, and the breeder was just being courteous by putting her up. Although it's not unusual for the sire of a litter to be owned by a second party and live elsewhere, if at all possible a prospective buyer should at least peek at fifty percent of their pup's genetic makeup.

This conversation took place nearly two years ago. Rooney has now grown into a truly beautiful specimen, and my sister's family couldn't be fonder of her. She is very loving towards every member of the family. She wrestles tenaciously with the family's older spaniel mix, and she tends to boss the cat around. All in all, she fit into Jean's household well. Outside of putting up a fight over nail trimming and being outwardly grouchy when they remove her from the couch (I'll address this type of protest behavior later in the book), Rooney is fairly respectful of her human family members. However, when it comes to outsiders, Rooney is my sister's first and last line of defense even though Jean wasn't in the market for any alarms or security guards.

On the very first holiday my sister hosted after acquiring Rachel's birthday gift, I heard a brand new ring to the doorbell. It sounded kind of like a WATCH DOG. When Jean opened the door holding her (I mean Rachel's) little badger dog, she didn't greet me with a traditional "Merry Christmas!" Instead of "How have you been?" I heard over Rooney's barking, "Isn't she adorable, she thinks she is so big!" The truth was Rooney did think she was big enough and old enough to take action when face to face with someone she didn't approve of. She was only about six months old that holiday, and she was already Dachshund enough to establish some policies. Rooney made it clear to her family early on, if she was uncomfortable with an outsider (whether at the vet's office or in her own living room) she wasn't becoming friendly anytime soon. After long minutes of exposure Rooney would eventually settle into a quiet state next to one of her family members, but as soon as the stranger stood up, walked across the room, or especially if this outsider initiated interaction, Rooney once again exploded into alarm.

My sister had envisioned taking little Rooney to her kids sporting events, but she found out early on that the more strangers there were, the more defensive Rooney became. Rooney was very much a puppy, and this meant she was bolder and more assertive within her own territory where she gained confidence from pack members and familiarity. But even at the ballpark, if my sister allowed or encouraged an admirer to offer a hand for petting, Rooney would lash out with a snap hoping to discourage any further attempts at making friends. Of course these incidents were embarrassing to Jean, so her Dachshund's social debut was short lived.

Months passed without me seeing little Rooney, and since I'd not heard anything from Jean about Dachshunds, hostility, or training I thought they must be doing well with their new family member. A few weeks before a large cookout that my sister and her husband host every year, Jean called to say that she was genuinely worried about having so many guests around her little watch dog. They had even gotten to the point where they put her away when certain guests came over, because with some people (probably the most offensive or manageable targets as Rooney assessed it) her barks were quickly turning into nips on the ankles.

For my sister, like nearly every family I work with, she intended to structure Rooney's life better than she had done. Jean did say that she meant to call me months prior to begin obedience training, but she thought there was still plenty of time. In such a short period, Rooney's defensiveness had moved so smoothly from a cute to a major problem that it completely caught Jean off guard. Jean and her husband, like most people, have a plate full of responsibilities. They are busy enough that months slip by almost unnoticed. As for me, busy or not, I had no excuse for not checking on my niece and her feisty birthday gift as I promised I would do. More than anyone, I knew Rooney's potential for defensiveness, and I knew it could be a time sensitive matter. **But I knew from a lifetime of dog training, it's never, ever too late to begin effective behavior shaping.** I would call it the rare month at the training center when we don't have a canine student enrolled who is substantially over ten years old.

For my niece's dog, official training began immediately after the phone call, and I went to their house on day one to lay a foundation of environmental structure. This structure is a critical first step in defensive dog control. Rooney had been a relatively easy pup to house train, and in general she was an easy dog. Those things considered, along with the fact that she was primarily an indoor dog, there had been little use made of leash, collar, and crate. That was about to change. New rules were in order, and they weren't subject to Rooney's approval. Here were the new training conditions for the blossoming watch dog: rule number one, if there were any visitors on the property (inside the house or out) Rooney needed to be supervised by a primary handler; rule number two, when she was supervised Rooney needed to be wearing a secure collar (preferably a working slip or similar collar) and attached to this collar would be a quality three/eighths inch, six foot leash that she would drag around or be held loosely in hand; rule number three, if non-family members were present on the property and no primary handler was able to supervise, Rooney would be safely stowed in a comfortable crate. My intention was to immediately take away all of the free, inappropriate opportunities for defensive action. Like me, Jean and her family actually appreciated their Dachshund's watch dog ability; they simply didn't want it carrying over to innocent parties. There is nothing wrong with Jeff (my Brother-in-Law) praising Rooney at the park for barking at a strange man who steps out from behind a tree and startles them. By the same token, if a sales woman rings the front doorbell and sets off the Dachshund alarm, there's nothing wrong with a little praise for the alert. However, if my Brother-in-Law wants to promote this justifiable defensive behavior, he needs also to build into his relationship with Rooney a shut off switch. This is exactly the plan Jeff wanted to follow, so on the first training day I needed to allow Rooney a brief alert opportunity (associated with a small amount of praise) then followed by a chosen quiet signal that is associated with self control handling. All this may seem like a tall order, but in training the steps flow together quite naturally.

As soon as we had set up new living conditions for Rooney it was time to adjust the rules of engagement. Effective handling in a defensive dog situation needs to begin the moment a canine student detects a stranger's presence. This means when the defensive dog walks within the proximity of an outsider or when the outsider approaches the dog's proximity, (whether that occurs in the living room or at the park) the handler must insist upon loose leash composure immediately after acknowledging a justifiable alert and issuing a quiet signal like "hush" (as taught in The Ten Natural Steps to Training the Family

Dog). If you are not inclined to encourage any defensive behavior, then canine self control should be insisted upon at the moment of alerting. Regardless of how you approach the experience, when composure is requested by the handler's plan, preventing the canine student from bothering anyone is critical. The handler should not allow any hostile display (lunging, growling, barking, or lip curling), and the handler should prevent the defensive canine from hiding behind legs or under furniture. This self control we reinforce needs to be carried out on a loose leash that is held securely in hand, smack dab in the middle of all the activity. The name of this game is hang out in the theater of engagement while simultaneously pushing for tolerance in the face of what used to be the hostile canine's targets.

The handler needs to hold a tough line. No threatening action can be tolerated on the dog's part. If the handler witnesses even a hint of assertive behavior from his student, a swift leash and collar tug needs to be administered. Assertive behavior may be described as pushing forward to smell, hard staring, or pressing against a stranger.

Since most defensive situations occur in relative close quarters, it's not uncommon for the hostile dog's initial response to be explosive. In regards to deterrents or negative consequences, this explosive start may force a handler to immediately administer an extended correction (as described in Chapter 2) to calm the student. Our objective here would be preventing the self rewarding, hysterical behavior from escalating and therefore perpetuating the unpleasant action. Using standard leash and collar tugs with an explosively hostile dog can add more fuel to an already roaring emotional fire. What we find at the training center, not only is a canine student's mind clouded (making it impossible for him to learn or process information) when he's in this hysterical state, his pain threshold also has been driven through the roof by this emotional explosion (not unlike his human counterparts). The high pain threshold and the clouded mind render standard leash and collar tugs useless. Time and time again, the extended correction has proven to us at the training center to be the best sedative and brain defogger at our disposal. In other words, the quickest approach to comfort, safety, and learning is a calming extended correction.

In a case of defensive behavior management as demonstrated by little Miss Rooney, the task at hand is to replace the proactive, take charge mindset (which leads to stimulating, self rewarding action) with a more passive, receptive one (which probably won't be as stimulating or self rewarding). So the moment a canine student shows effort towards self restraint or handler deference, the handler must acknowledge this with genuine, soothing praise and a reassuring touch. Without removing the excitement and manipulative effects of hostile behavior and without a fat paycheck for exhausting self control, a handler will have a very hard time selling his intelligent canine friend on an aggression management plan. Applying meaningful, timely deterrents (firm leash and collar tugs or extended corrections) and offering meaningful, timely incentives is the only way to end up with dependable aggression control. **Timely is an important word in this behavior shaping plan. Allowing a dog to get carried away in his hostility for any time at all makes it more difficult to bring him back to passivity.** On that same note, failing to reward a defensive dog for a small outward move toward restraint makes it very unlikely he will exert more effort for larger moves. Astute observations are needed to be timely, so try not to let your guard drop when you're acting as a primary handler.

Taking notice of the dog's effort is a pivotal task for a handler, because outward effort reflects the inward mindset. As handlers, if we demonstrate to the dog-in-training that we know where he is going with an idea and we'll act accordingly, we are shaping the way this student thinks under certain conditions. This line of thought leads to a simple dog training truth: we must change the way a canine student thinks about a situation before we can expect a change in the way he independently chooses to act in that same situation. I chose the word "independent" on purpose, because my long-term training goal is for the dog to provide a pleasing, autonomous action. As a handler, I'm free to work or play with my canine teammate instead of ride herd over him and monitor his every move.

The first day of training for Rooney unfolded in an orderly fashion. I arranged to be in my sister's living room acting as the primary handler. Rooney had already been wearing her leash and collar, (dragging it around the house) for about thirty minutes before a prearranged guest knocked on the front

Defensive Aggression

door. According to Jeff's wishes (mine too), I followed Rooney's initial barking over the door knock with a soothing "Good girl." Remember, very little praise is needed at the initial alarm with an enthusiastic watch dog, because the explosive expression itself is rewarding. In the next step, I uttered the brand new signal "Hush." Keep in mind, Rooney has no clue what I want with this word, so at this point only gentle leash tugs are all I use to direct her attention around to me. When she ceased barking (albeit for the briefest of moments) to look back at me, I said to her "Good girl, hush!" Of course, Rooney much preferred her watch dog duties to pleasing me, so she went right back at barking. This time I followed with stronger repeated leash tugs, when she again quieted (looking at me), I repeated, "Good girl, hush!" It took another cycle of this before she sustained being quiet, and all the while the guest was still outside the closed door occasionally repeating the knocking.

A common error that new handlers make is having the guest advance to the inside before control over the dog is reached. Avoid this trap, and do not put more on the plate than either the dog or the handler can manage. If you choose not to use a hush command, follow the same cycle simply omitting the word. As a side note, do not beat your dog up with the hush signal; it should not be used as a reprimand. "Hush" as used here is a positive word associated with being quiet or relaxed. At the training center when we work on aggression control or general obedience, we really don't make use of negative words or negative emotion. At this quiet moment with Rooney, I also insist on legitimate composure that includes: maintaining a loose leash and refraining from jumping on me or the door. In other words, I expect general self control without any formal command reinforcement. Once Rooney was able to manage her composure responsibility it was time for step two, opening the door. As soon as the door opened, my little watch dog caught sight of the guest and exploded into another barking fit. At this point I no longer used the hush signal. I'd already established the policy of accepting this guest and it was in force for the duration of this visit. I used the leash and collar at once to quash the barking. She was persistent in her threats toward the unwanted visitor that she could now clearly see only two feet away. I had to be just as persistent with the non verbal leash and collar tugs. To make a successful step forward in this training exercise I would have to match Rooney's tenacity in confronting the outsider with my own determination to have her greet the guest passively. Until she acquiesced, the visit did not move forward. Simply stated: there was no communication between the visitor and me or the visitor and Rooney, Rooney was not allowed to display hostility toward the visitor, the visitor was instructed not to move forward, and Rooney was not allowed to move forward. The visitor was instructed not to retreat from the stoop, and I would not allow Rooney to retreat from the proximity of activity.

At this pivotal moment, I was proving to Rooney her aggressive behavior was no longer profitable. The stranger was not going to retreat, there was no satisfaction for her from a hysterical hostile display, she was not going to be picked up and pampered for her unwanted behavior, and she was not going to be able to escape from this close encounter with an outsider. The best way I have found to raise a defensive dog's comfort level around strangers is to arrange frequent opportunities (multiple per week) for the right kind of exposure (orchestrated by the handler) over an extended period of time (several months). Demonstrating to Rooney that the team leader controlled the environment, the outsiders, and her behavior worked wonders in the very first training exercise. Both Jeff and Jean commented on the visible relief they instantly noticed as Rooney gave into the inevitable new policies. She was being relieved of her inherent and somewhat stressful watch dog responsibility. She was being relieved of the panic to escape. Rooney was also being relieved of the urges to seek out an aggression high. All in all, her new team leader stepped in and dramatically simplified her life.

When Rooney was exposed to different, justifiable, defensive situations, I would again apply the hush command followed up with praise if she quieted or tugging with leash and collar if she didn't. I would continue this cycle until we were successful. In situations where a defensive dog displays hostility towards illegitimate targets such as a nonthreatening child at the park or a neighbor (minding his own business) cutting the grass, I give no hush signal in these circumstances. Instead, I jump immediately to leash and collar tugs as a deterrent for this unwanted behavior. I want to send a very clear message to the canine student that this kind of action is never acceptable when directed towards these types of targets.

Rooney wasn't terribly concerned with any threat as long as it was a safe distance away. She was purely defensive in her actions, and she didn't care much about patrolling territory or guarding spaces. If a threat wasn't closing in on her personal zone, she was content to let things be. This kind of indifference sometimes sent the wrong signal to a passerby who was taken aback by the seemingly passive little dog who turned into a monster when they approached to pet her. This was especially true as she learned to disengage from her hostile behavior towards strangers in order to please her handler. With the newly acquired self control, Rooney was more attractive than ever to outsiders. So this means, as the primary handler, one of my jobs was to keep the visitor (who had just stepped through the doorway) from overstepping their boundaries and engaging the cute little Dachshund. I needed a clear demonstration for Rooney that an unpleasant (as she assessed) stranger would not take advantage of her lowered defenses by trying to pet or pick her up. Even face to face sweet talk can be received by a defensive canine as confrontational. Too many times, I've heard dog owners trying to lower their pet's defenses by forcing physical contact between their natural born watch dog and outsiders. In this often futile attempt to build a friendship, battle lines are drawn instead. The objective is to allow a defensive dog the time and the space she needs (to accept an outsider to the best of her innate ability). Defensive canines accept or reject strangers by degree. Some staunchly on-guard pets may never be comfortable with a visitor regardless of the frequency or duration of encounters. We also see regularly those family watch dogs, who after the initial controlled greeting with any stranger the dog will honestly befriend them.

A story I use all the time to put things in perspective for defensive dog owners is the story of my two close friends Amy and Mike. I would like to invite them both over for dinner occasionally, but there's a snag. Mike really likes Amy, but she finds him repulsive and irritating. To remedy the situation, I need to improve their relations so I formulate two different plans for this purpose. To begin each plan I invite both Amy and Mike over to watch a ball game, and I have Mike show up early so we can go over the two outlines. The first strategy is explaining to Mike how Amy finds him repulsive, so while we watch the ball game I want him to sit next to her on the couch and put his arm around her shoulder. I also want Mike to whisper jokes into her ear during the game while he feeds her chips. So in other words, work hard to win her over. If the first strategy fails (I can't imagine how!) we'll shift immediately to our default scenario. In this second plan I have Mike take a polar opposite approach to Amy. If she sits on the couch, I want Mike to sit in an adjacent chair. I do not want Mike to force conversation with Amy. If she engages him in conversation, I want Mike to respond politely and briefly. If he goes to the kitchen to get something to eat or drink, offer to bring something back for her. With this strategy Mike needs to be respectful, give Amy space, and essentially leave her alone.

You don't have to be a psychologist or a professional dog trainer to imagine where each scenario may lead. If Amy truly finds Mike irritating, having more of him right on top of her will only magnify the hard feelings and increase her dread over the next repulsive encounter. We won't even get into the possibilities of Amy being hostile and successfully running Mike off. On the other hand, lessening the irritation through minimal contact and engagement will in turn reduce the dread of the next encounter.

I took the liberty to anthropomorphize with this story, because it really has helped my clients to understand their defensive dog's perspective through Amy. At the training center, we find that the second strategy works almost without exception to reduce a defensive canine's hostility and increase acceptance of outsiders. The first strategy usually leads to more intense aggression when a defensive dog is confronted with yet another repulsive or irritating (as the dog sees it) intruder.

Defensive Aggression

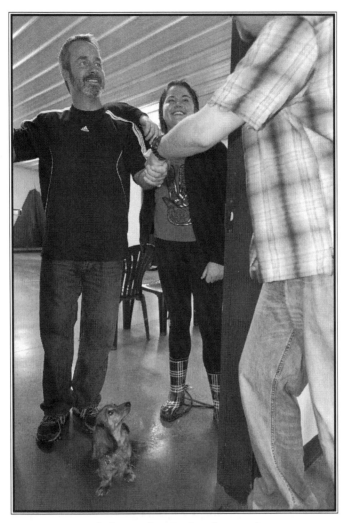

Little Rooney keeping her alarm under
control while greeting a visitor

Once Rooney had accepted the presence of the stranger inside the house, all of us (Jeff, Jean, Rooney, the visitor, and me) moved to the living room for a normal sit down chat. Of course, I insisted on the little watch dog's composure (loose leash, handler proximity, and self control) throughout the visit even as we intentionally played musical chairs. Rooney accepted the new challenges like she had been expected to all her life, with no more than a single leash and collar tug (for growling at the guest) when we first stood up to change seats. By the time most dogs get to the living room and musical chairs portion of this training exercise, they have conceded to the handler's wishes of visitor tolerance.

I want you to remember back to the statements I made about effort in the right or wrong direction. In no part of dog training do I ever expect a student to be perfect. The process of dog training is a shaping process. We are adjusting canine behavior, not changing canine personalities. I made it clear to my sister and brother-in-law, Rooney will probably never like most of the visitors that come to the house, and that's OK! She doesn't have to like them; she just needs to tolerate them. When I was working with Rooney on her first training day, I was forgiving when she turned her head away from the visitor and growled under her breath, all on loose leash close to me. What an improvement that was over lunging and barking at the intruder. I believed that she could and would do better, but at this point in training her behavior modification represented a monumental effort in the right direction. **A huge effort in the right direction, yet she was still displaying hostility over the presence of the guest (effort in the wrong direction). How should a primary handler respond in a situation like this? The answer is, neutrally. I neither praised nor corrected Rooney in that long moment.** I waited instead for a more decisive behavioral movement. Either her focus would turn more confrontationally toward the visitor, or she would relax even further bringing an end to the growling.

In Rooney's case, she chose to melt onto the floor and nearly fall asleep, only occasionally eyeballing the guest with no display of hostility. So I was able to follow my neutral response with genuinely soothing praise. I do mean soothing or calming praise as opposed to stimulating or encouraging. In these challenging moments when a dog is using all of their inherent tools to cap their own drive and energy, the last thing a new student needs at a time like this is more (infused) enthusiasm. Reward without added excitement is what I wanted to give Rooney. So a single relaxing stroke and a tidbit of food is what she received for all her effort. Had her growl escalated or her posture turned (even a little) more threatening, I would have swiftly impressed her with a leash and collar action in order to move one step closer to a mindset of acceptance by quashing her aggressive displays toward this particular visitor.

Rooney's first training session ended with the calm living room visit. I wanted her to walk away from this experience with a pleasant taste in her mouth and important concepts on her mind. Training day number two for the mighty Dachshund was the very next afternoon. I was determined not to have any more time lapse between sessions than was absolutely necessary, because momentum is a critical factor in the aggression control equation.

My sister, and Rooney (carrying a lingering memory of the previous day's lesson on stranger tolerance) met me at a small local park for the second training experience. Once more, I made arrangements for a (different) stranger of choice to enter Rooney's personal space. In this scenario, Jean was acting as the primary handler and I tagged along as her coach. Our plan was to casually hike down one of the main trails in the park while working on Rooney's loose leash walking skills. At a predetermined trail crossing our passive stranger was going to walk up to us and ask for directions. The quality of a training experience often times hinges on the thought and energy a handler puts into preparation. Jean and her watch dog were actually exposed to a very similar situation like this not long before we began training (my sister described the encounter as hysterical embarrassment), so as we neared the pre-planned meeting spot Jean grew tighter and tighter as if anticipating a guerilla ambush.

My sister's anxiety over the anticipated meeting just added to the realism as far as Rooney was concerned, because that was the normal mood that hung over her handlers when out for a stroll. Rooney didn't give their mood a second thought because the hostile explosions they viewed with dread she saw as nothing but stimulating. To Rooney, encountering the enemy meant energizing action, and until the first training lesson she couldn't see a down side to the hostile explosion. The intense expression felt good, manipulating outsiders was satisfying, and she would usually receive extra attention from her family members in their attempts to calm her. All these positive reinforcers that she connected to defensive encounters only made her hungrier for more. That's why from the moment they stepped out of the car, Jean had such a difficult time convincing Rooney to walk on loose leash.

When we reached the designated trail juncture our hiking stranger walked up right on time. I had been preparing Jean from the start of our walk to allow Rooney an initial barking alert (since Jean and Jeff both agreed they want a little bit of watch dog behavior), as long as she maintained a loose leash on my sister's left side (the proper walking position). After the initial alert, I instructed Jean to give Rooney a "hush" command and allow her a full one, one thousand count to respond. If Rooney did cease with barking, I told Jean to immediately give her all three kinds of reward (physical petting, genuine verbal praise, and a tidbit of food reward). That would have been no small victory to accomplish such a degree of responsiveness in such a short period of time. My sister and I also talked extensively about the more probable outcome where Rooney doesn't even acknowledge Jean's existence after a quiet command. In that case the plan for my sister, after a one, one thousand count following the command, (assuming Rooney is still displaying hostility) was to quietly administer strong enough leash and collar tugs to pull Rooney's attention around to the handler. Once that is accomplished and the little watch dog tunes out the stranger to focus on the handler (if only for a moment), pay her immediately for that self control effort.

Regardless of Rooney's reaction, the stranger on the trail, just like the stranger the day before at the house, was going to be absolutely nonreactive to Rooney's behavior. **Hence, like all the training scenarios I've described so far, I want an informed helper who will follow instruction to pose as the stranger, the visitor, the passerby, etc. In these early training situations we can't afford to give an aggressive dog the wrong message (outsiders are frightening and dangerous), an accidental reward for inappropriate behavior (strangers retreat or acquiesce in the face of hostility), or an unplanned disincentive for appropriate effort (when defenses are lowered visitors make you feel uncomfortable by moving into your personal space).** Later, after seasoning and proofing a canine student around distraction possibilities, exposure to the unpredictability of real life is absolutely necessary. Less than desirable outcomes to certain instruction scenarios will not be as detrimental to the overall training program at this point.

Rooney did charge out to the end of her leash and sound off toward the stranger at first sight. Jean really surprised me and stuck to her guns with no additional encouragement from me. It took her several sharp leash tugs to back Rooney off, but once she accomplished that the Dachshund held pretty well to loose leash self control. A few quiet moments allowed Jean to stoop down to Rooney's level and reward her sufficiently. When the praising was over, Jean stood up and engaged in some conversation with the acting stranger, afterwards each continued hiking in their own direction down the path. Once Rooney had deferred to Jean there was only one other test when the stranger passed by relatively close to us. The little watch dog was challenged to keep her mind on the loose leash and her close to the handler position, but she did it quietly.

There is no doubt that this potentially negative encounter was mitigated a great deal by the fresh learning experiences that Rooney benefitted from the previous day. The understandings and responsibilities the Dachshund gleaned from earlier training gave her a novel sense of right and wrong, which led to less commitment and determination in this day's defensive pursuits. This growing sensitivity to the handler's wishes made it possible for my sister (who was reluctant to be Rooney's disciplinarian) to be an effective team leader with only minimal resistance from her cute couch buddy. **Momentum really makes a difference!**

Having Jean or Jeff handle Rooney as soon as possible was an important step in controlling her defensiveness. Most family dogs gain courage from the presence of important pack members. So in essence, Rooney's hostile behavior was more intense and therefore more difficult to control in my sister's company. All the more reason to set up this realistic encounter with Jean at the helm to ensure our training approach was going to be successful in the natural environment without my presence. Also, the confidence my sister gained from actually being instrumental in Rooney's control was priceless for future application. At my training center, all dog training (especially aggression control) is centered on the owner's instruction and handling.

Rooney's training moved along very quickly from the park scenario, owing greatly to the fact she was still young and quite malleable. My role in her instruction also diminished rapidly, because Jean and Jeff (much to my delight and surprise) proved to be quick studies and very capable handlers. On their own, they set up successive training experiences in multiple environments that incorporated strangers or guests that gradually increased the challenge and realism for Rooney. As the bar of expectation is slowly raised for a canine student, the owner's policies must remain in place and the handling must remain consistent. After a defensive canine becomes comfortable and dependable with the self control concept, utilizing a formal command like down or stay (assuming they're properly trained to do so) or offering a pacifier (a bone or toy) as a follow up, is perfectly acceptable at this point in training. By this time our message has been clearly delivered to the dog, hostile behavior needs to be managed through self control. As primary handlers, you should not want or need a crutch like a formal command or a ball to skirt around unacceptable behavior. However, directing the mind of an already composed student onto something more positive is a good maneuver.

Chapter Six

Territorial Aggression

What is the difference between defensive and territorial aggression? For the purpose of selecting the optimal aggression management strategy, I separate these two forms of hostile expression by the importance a dog places on perimeter. Even though these two types of behavior are often overlapping, there is a distinction in motive for the purist of either category and that distinction determines how the handler should orchestrate the training effort. Sometimes a defensive dog has only a small desire, and therefore devotes little energy to patrolling an area or ridding familiar ground of outsiders. In the case of my sister's dog, if a stranger wasn't actually moving into Rooney's personal space she was content to let them pass on by. On the other hand, I frequently work with exuberantly territorial canines that easily accept and even enjoy the company of guests or strangers once these outsiders have crossed the perimeter and entered the area. The thrill for a dog like this is keeping his designated area (as he defines the area) clean of outsiders. But once a challenge has passed (a guest made entry, a passerby passed, or a delivery person returned to the truck), he's looking forward to the next opportunity to protect the perimeter. However, more times than not a watch dog that avidly gets into his role will be both territorial and defensive. I often describe this kind of guardian as a canine with a very large personal space! In other words, to an energetic or driven watch dog, space is space and he enjoys keeping it all clean of those bothersome outsiders that don't belong.

Just like Rooney the defensive Dachshund, territorial dogs are born with this passion to protect their home area against invasion. One of the first concepts I discuss with the owner's of a home guardian is satisfaction. The canine patroller is not only exhilarated by the potential confrontations with intruders, but the urges to rid home space of danger are satisfied (therefore he's gratified) every time he's successful at keeping outsiders out. So the first step in controlling a dog's aggression in circumstances like these is to remove the rush of hostile exhilaration and the feeling of satisfaction gained from his action. Not unlike the defensive encounters I outlined with my sister's Dachshund, control of the environment and the outcome of the event must be implemented. Territorial situations can be more challenging for a handler to manage due to a greater working area and the difficulty in setting up training scenarios.

It can be very trying for a primary handler to administer the appropriate timely consequences for a territorial dog's actions because the event often occurs with the canine student in a separate location from that of the team captain. There is no simple management plan when the dog is guarding the fenced yard against the next door neighbor and the handler is in the house having dinner. If a watch dog is loose in the house running from window to window keeping mail carriers, delivery people, and passersby at bay while the primary handler is at work, there is no possibility for shaping his behavior away from this stimulating and satisfying action. **In most cases, one of the only ways to remove the rush and gratification of territorial hostility is to remove the opportunity. No matter how hard a handler works to control this type of aggression while he's present with the dog, if the free opportunities (when the dog is on his own) are not removed the undesirable behavior will persist.** Like all the other forms of hostility we cover in this book, fruitful display of territorial aggression is reinforcing and therefore self perpetuating. When the mail carrier fails to make entry into the house, when the delivery person retreats to the truck, or when the neighbor keeps his distance, the area guardian sees it as mission accomplished.

It's paramount in the management of territorial aggression to have a clear understanding of the defined area from a canine's perspective. Obviously, the average watch dog views tangible barriers around larger areas like fencing and house walls as dividing lines between outsiders and insiders, but smaller spaces like pens, crates, and vehicles can also be described as an inside separated from an outside. Even a fixed radius like a dog fastened to an anchored tether or connected to a leash held in hand designates an area either inside or outside the radius of ranging motion. If a bold and confident territorial canine is given the freedom to set his own boundaries because no tangible barriers exist, then he will probably eagerly patrol all the area within eyesight if not within the greater limits of what he hears. This is the reason why in residentially or commercially developed regions, tangible barriers or handler supervision is mandatory for the proper management of territorial watch dogs. Legal property lines don't mean anything to animals. The small plots laid out for an average size neighborhood or city block easily overlap in a dog's mind, so what the territorial canine detects are outsiders living and working in his area. In other words, the neighbor next door or the mail carrier down the street can all represent the enemy at the gate for an overly zealous guardian.

To begin behavior shaping with a territorial dog, select the smallest area with an important perimeter where both you and the canine student can comfortably interact. A good place to start in some cases is sitting in a parked vehicle as a passenger or the driver while the watch dog hangs out on the back seat, cargo area, or crate. A commonly guarded but manageable territory to work in is the living room or closed porch with windows for outside viewing. The next venue of choice would be a small fenced in yard (hopefully closed in by a tangible barrier rather than the buried signal wire type), the smaller the better. More times than I like, I'm recruited to work with an outside dog that patrols a large open expanse, a nearly impossible situation to get a grip on.

In any of these scenarios, realistic helpers are needed to pose as intruders or outsiders. Coordinating the time and intensity of the stranger's approach is necessary for effective action on the handler's part. Controlling the environment to reduce the chances of interference and mishaps is just as important here as it has been through all the aggression work so far. Having training collars and leashes in place and at the ready before any outsider approaches the designated territory is critical for training success. The primary handler must be prepared to administer the appropriate consequence in connection to the dog's action when the action occurs. These are the reasons why small, contained areas are desirable for territorial aggression work and large, open areas are not.

I'm going to tell you the story of "Pi" (aka, 3.14), a ten month old English Mastiff that belongs to my good friend John. Pi is very well bred, and John went to a great deal of trouble to find a Mastiff of her caliber. She is my friend's third Mastiff, but the first to demonstrate legitimate hostility towards human beings. John is very active with his dogs and for the last eight years has traveled extensively competing with them in conformation and obedience trials. As a side note, he's been very successful with championships and high in trial scores under his belt. So John is no novice when it comes to dog handling, but he never had to deal with one of his dogs threatening people until his sweet little Pi came along. She really does have a sweet and happy nature about her except when it comes to John's van, her traveling home. Pi is well into her obedience training and interacts with people very well, as long as they don't get too close to the family vehicle. We've seen happy, social Pi regularly at the training center since she was three months old, so it was hard for me to imagine her barking and growling out the van window at a passerby. Although it was hard to imagine, I knew John was dog savvy and seriously concerned about Pi's competition career with this newly born hostility coming on, so we wasted no time in setting up a training scenario.

Realism being the key to long term training success, we set up the first stranger to approach John's van while he was parked down the road from the training center in an empty parking lot. I did not want Pi to have any notions about obedience, the training center, or me. I was planning for a genuine aggressive showing on her part, so we could quickly impress her with strong leash and collar action. This hopefully would set up forever in her mind the association between territorial hostility and negative consequences. In the past, John had been caught off guard by Pi's hostile displays. He tried to quash the unwanted behavior with reprimands and one hand grabs on her collar while sitting in the front seat of his parked van. These meager attempts at dissuasion had little effect on the strong minded Mastiff. In fact, John's emotional stimulation only added to Pi's aggressive exhilaration. This additional excitement coupled with higher confidence gained from experience and maturation, was quickly transforming young Pi into a formidable area guardian. Unlike my sister and brother-in-law, John wanted no part of owning a watch dog. His life with dogs centered on social activities and competitions where he saw no room for any kind of hostility. From that perspective, John didn't want to praise Pi for a moment when she jumped into watch dog mode. He didn't want to develop a hush command. He didn't want a guardian at all. What he needed was that aggressive switch shut off as securely as possible.

For Pi's next territorial opportunity, John was more prepared. The van was running but in park, he had a leash already hooked to Pi's training collar, and his seat belt was off so both arms were free for impressive leash and collar action. John's mouth was theoretically taped shut so no negative emotions were going to fuel Pi's fire and he knew exactly when and where the stranger would appear. The stranger (my daughter, Heidi) was instructed not to react to the watch dog's antics. Our plan was very simple and natural, Heidi was going to approach John's van and ask for directions on the passenger side at the rear door where Pi rides. The van windows were in their customary half open position so that our territorial Mastiff could see and hear anything that approached her small mobile area while John appeared busy talking on his phone. As for me, I was watching from a distance with binoculars, so I was virtually inside the van studying Pi's behavior and John's handling techniques. The template for training success boils down to goal attainment through detail management, in other words, instruction orchestration.

Here's how the sequence of events unfolded. Heidi approached the parked vehicle as planned. As she closed in on the rear passenger window, Pi was alerted and slowly moved towards the opening. When Pi first focused on Heidi, I had instructed John to stealthily take hold of the leash so he would be ready for a correction at the exact moment he detected the slightest hostility. What we hoped for was an early, strong negative consequence that would instantaneously shut the aggressive behavior down and simultaneously redirect Pi's focus toward John. Given Pi's youth and her newness to the watch dog role, along with the fact that John was using a leverage collar (pinch collar) on his powerful companion, we had a good chance to permanently alter her behavior with this one experience. As Heidi began to speak, Pi began to grumble and John perfectly administered three sharp leash and collar tugs. Just like clockwork, Pi shut down her hostile display and backed away from the window to focus on her handler. Heidi held her ground and never missed a beat asking John for directions. John coolly gave Heidi what she needed, and Pi learned an invaluable lesson. Pi's territorial aggression no longer kept strangers at bay, her hostile display no longer stimulated John, and in the place of the onetime satisfying effects she received a very unpleasant consequence.

John is able to visit with Heidi now that "Pi" has her territorial tendency under wraps

Even in the training sessions to follow, we were unable to entice Pi into any kind of hostile display. As my friend John will attest, one well orchestrated and impressive experience can permanently shape behavior. On a side note, Pi's youth and inexperience along with the use of the leverage collar made this onetime fix possible. Even though most territorial aggression won't be curbed this quickly, persistence and diligence with a similar approach will win the day in the vast majority of cases.

The training challenge increases in direct correlation with the increase of territory. I'm going to move our training strategy into a fenced back yard of modest size. A classic situation comes to mind with Aztec, my co-worker's (Katherine) seven year old Australian shepherd. Katherine and her husband recently purchased a home with a modest sized fenced in yard. Although moving into noisy suburbia from the quiet country was a big change for the entire family, it was especially challenging for Aztec since he was used to wide open spaces (his territory as far as he could see) and having no neighbors. As a mature dog set in his very comfortable ways, Katherine's Aussie had a lot to get used to. He had never, in his seven years, been restricted to such a small area. He definitely never had to manage regular outsiders so close to the den before moving to the neighborhood. Katherine truthfully didn't even know her Aussie had territorial tendencies until the first afternoon he was turned loose in the fenced yard.

When clients at the training center meet Aztec, the universal response is that he is a sweet and friendly dog; and I think that is the best way to describe him. He has the best of manners, and he's genuinely affectionate even with strangers at the park or the vet's office. Now if you walk up on Aztec's back yard you're going to see a different side of Katherine's companion, a hostile aspect that she had never seen until their move. Unfortunately for Katherine, her next door neighbors tend to be busy outdoor people, and to compound matters the common fence between their yards is chain link so Aztec can see everything they do. In an attempt to ease her watch dog's mind, Katherine set up introductions between Aztec and the neighbors. For the first visit, she walked him over to their house and the second time she had them come to her back yard. On both occasions, the neighbors saw sweet and friendly Aztec. Like me, Katherine typically does not allow other people to feed her dog, but in this situation she was going to do all she could to be the pleasant new kid on the block.

None of that worked, of course, or I wouldn't be writing about Katherine's dog in this section of this book. I think she did all the right things, and with some milder canine personalities, the visit and food experiences may mitigate the guarding tendency. Aztec, however, took his job of guarding that small territory very seriously. So after the visit and treats experience, Aztec was back on the job at the first opportunity to charge the fence barking and lunging any time the neighbors dared to open their back door. All of us who were involved with this situation agreed, Aztec probably would not follow through with his threats and actually bite someone who reached over the fence. However, the hostile alarm was annoying for Katherine's neighbors, who missed the peace of their back yard and really didn't like worrying about being grabbed by their new neighbor's watch dog.

What should Katherine do about Aztec? There was no simple answer for this question. The best approach to managing her territorial dog was to move out of the neighborhood and back to the country. Since that wasn't an option, several remedies were employed. Putting up a privacy fence at least down the sides of the yard would visually shield Aztec from adjacent, neighbor activity. She should arrange most of his free time in the back yard to coincide with lowest activity of the adjacent neighbors. Whenever possible, arrange supervised time out in the back yard for Aztec, which would coincide with neighbor activity (this way Katherine or her husband would be available to supply consequences in accordance with Aztec's behavior). Develop a hush command during this supervised time so Aztec could become accustomed to the idea of neighbor activity and quiet tolerance. Finally, keep up the friendly neighbor visits so gradually the outsiders feel more like insiders (this final step was only appropriate because Katherine and her husband genuinely liked their next door neighbors and wished to foster a closer relationship with them).

The most challenging aspect of Aztec's training plan for Katherine (besides the laborious task of putting up a privacy fence) was being able to supply effective negative consequences for her dog's inappropriate aggressive behavior while he was free to roam in the yard. Dogs with the liberty to patrol their yards create a major challenge in every territorial case. There are only a few solutions to this conundrum. If a primary handler is inside the house when his watch dog explodes into territorial aggression while on patrol in the fenced yard, and if the hush command is desired and developed as I describe in the Defensive aggression chapter, then the handler must be available to deliver a hush command. If, however, a handler simply wants to quash the territorial behavior without preserving any allowance for alarm, then the handler must walk out to the hostile canine and deliver an effective correction. When a negative consequence is necessary, the primary handler must walk out to his dog and connect a leash to the working collar (that the canine student should already be wearing) and deliver sharp tugs. In this particular scenario, the handler is inside and only intermittently checking on the dog that is outside. So for safety reasons, the leash should not be attached to the dog's collar and left to drag around as could be done with our constant supervision (like I've described in the Predatory aggression chapter). Assuming that a hush command is clearly understood by the territorial dog-in-training, if at any time he blatantly ignores this directive, the appropriate action is to follow through with the same kind of negative consequence.

Alternatively, if assuming the handler can be out in the yard (appearing busy) while his watch dog is free to patrol the fenced area, the management of territorial aggression in this situation is very similar to the approach I outlined in a previous chapter in the example of Roscoe interacting with cyclists or squirrels. Place a long line on the dog-in-training before he's turned loose in the fenced yard, because we don't want the long line to end up being the focus of the dog's attention while he's out in the yard. Good off-leash behavior is where we're headed, so don't call any more attention to the long line than necessary. Since we're operating in a fenced area with this scenario, we can be much more relaxed about the dog dragging the line around without the worry of him getting to the quarry before we secure the line for an effective correction. **Remember, in any hostile situation where you're the primary handler and your canine student requires a negative consequence- don't dally!** The more naturally driven a dog is to be hostile, the more rewarded he is during this kind of expression. Truncate the aggressive activity as soon as possible. In Aztec's situation, even though he's in a fenced yard and there's little danger of innocent outsiders getting hurt, Katherine still should not waste time in delivering a negative consequence to curb this behavior.

It was definitely easy for Katherine to be effective when she was out in the yard while her watch dog drug around a long line. She would give Aztec a single "hush" any time he alerted on the next door neighbors. Being the decisive and experienced trainer that she is, Katherine would not accept even a little huff after her directive, before she would deliver a correction with the long line. Given that Aztec wasn't that bent towards hostility any way, it took him no time to accept the neighbors along the fence line when his team leader was in the yard with him. It was a different story if Katherine was inside. Aztec put together two different sets of rules. The first was the quiet acceptance of neighbors whenever Katherine was in the yard with him. The second was to bark and get rowdy if he was unattended, because he realized when Katherine wasn't in the yard with him during some hostile expressions, the negative consequence was much slower in coming. Sometimes it didn't come at all (when Katherine was otherwise occupied), and this meant long periods of satisfaction guarding the fence line.

Just as most of us with territorial dogs and neighbors have to do, Katherine began working on several solutions simultaneously. Aztec's territorial aggression hung on for weeks, because of the free, exhilarating opportunities he was afforded when his team leader wasn't around. In many cases where canine family members persist in taking advantage of their fenced yard freedoms, a third solution for delivering timely, negative consequences in association with their unwanted watch dog behavior is the best option. Moving up to high tech equipment can be the most effective and the least negative training plan for a situation like Aztec's. There are two specific products I'm referring to in solution three. The battery powered, vocal cord activated bark-diminishing collar (different models from different manufacturers) and the battery powered, remote transmitter along with a receiving collar (again, many models from several manufactures). A battery powered pinch or bite is what a dog receives as a negative consequence when these products are activated. This same kind of deterrent is used with the popular, signal wire underground fence systems.

There are several advantages to the bark diminishing collars (Katherine's choice for Aztec by the way). The most important feature of this collar, once it's properly fitted to the dog, is that it doesn't require a handler for operation. The dog-in-training's sustained (an important word in this description), vocal cord vibration will activate a trigger that delivers a battery powered pinch where the collar's contact points rest against the dog's neck. A high quality version of this collar will usually be self setting through several stimulation levels. The automatic adjustment aspect of the collar allows the canine student's persistence and inherent toughness to determine the optimal stimulation level. These bark-diminishing collars are typically water tight so they can be worn rain or shine. All these features lead to the delivery of a handler free, negative consequence whenever the dog-in-training engages in sustained (a few moments, not a single bark, cough or sneeze) barking or growling. At the same time, a canine student wearing this collar is free to enjoy the back yard like he always has, as long as he doesn't break the excessive barking rule. So in Aztec's case, once Katherine made her policy of minimal watch dog behavior clear (using traditional leash and collar techniques), she was now free to simply put on Aztec's new self setting, battery powered, bark diminishing collar. She let this high tech product continue to reinforce the "no harassing the neighbors" rule while she was inside taking a nap. If, for whatever reason, Katherine wants Aztec to be able to express himself fully as a backyard watch dog (a burglar at large in the neighborhood, etc.), all she has to do is leave the bark diminishing collar off when she turns her guardian out in the yard.

This consideration brings up the point of equipment awareness. When it comes to the leash, long line, and remote control collar systems, I want those tools to disappear in the dog's mind as training moves forward. My goal is usually equipment free control, but not always. There are those times when I want a dog to be equipment aware. For example, a harness for my dog means a tracking adventure is at hand, and the sight of a flat collar excites my companion in preparation for scent detection work. In most cases, I believe it is acceptable for a dog to connect the idea of no sustained barking with the bark-diminishing collar, just like Katherine arranged with Aztec.

The remote control collar systems are also very effective tools when it comes to territorial aggression management. This product however, does require the full attention of the primary handler no differently than the use of a leash or long line. There is no automatic trigger for the typical remote collar system. A handler must push a button in order for a canine student to receive a battery powered bite. Although there is a wide range of stimulation levels, this type of training system requires the handler to select the optimal level best suited for the dog and the situation at hand. Reading the training booklet that comes with the purchase of one of these collars is a must. If any question remains about the operation of the unit, that wasn't sufficiently answered by the accompanying instruction, call an experienced professional trainer before an attempt is made to use the collar. The advantages of the remote control systems are great: the physicality of the correction is removed altogether, timing of the deterrent delivery can approach exactness, the intensity of a negative consequence can be adjusted higher or lower in less than a moment, and a canine student's distance (within reason) from the team leader does not undermine deterrent effectiveness. A handler, for instance, could be inside having dinner at the dining room table while watching the dog-in-training through a sliding glass door. If, in Katherine's case for example, Aztec launched into inappropriate watch dog mode during the family dinner, Katherine could deliver a perfectly timed and effective negative consequence without leaving her seat. Of course, if Katherine witnessed significant effort on Aztec's part to calmly walk away from neighbor activity, it would be worth disrupting dinner to open the door and offer a little praise.

As far as Katherine and Aztec were concerned, the bark diminishing collar was a perfect solution for their specific territorial problem. Since Aztec was already clear on his team leader's policy, further explanations weren't necessary. All Katherine needed was consistency in delivering negative consequences in association with the undesirable behavior. Aztec routinely wore his new collar in the back yard unless he was supervised by Katherine or her husband. Instantly, the consistency lacking in Katherine's behavior shaping plan was now in place. Whenever Aztec's neighbors ventured outside, tolerance and harmony was insisted upon by Katherine, her husband, or the bark-diminishing collar. Remember, Katherine desired some watch dog behavior from Aztec. So whenever the next door neighbors first appeared, she and her husband as well as the new collar allowed their guardian to make a little noise. It's only the relentless barking they wanted in check. As a side note, Katherine and her family have been in their new home about a year. They did eventually install a privacy fence that when coupled with the consistent follow through in their training plan, enabled Aztec to be peacefully collar-free in his back yard while the neighbors were peacefully busy in theirs. The entire process took several months, a worthwhile investment for good neighbors.

Once told to hush, Aztec must allow neighbors to hang on the fence

And then there was Stony, one dangerous dog! He was two years old when Cathy and I went to his house to film some in-home training. Stony was quite a specimen. Although not overly large for a Great Dane, he was well muscled and athletic. Confident and very aggressive, Stony was one of those rare dogs that make me feel uncomfortable. He was born "on guard" and truly formidable. He had already bitten a few people and nearly destroyed a couple of neighbor dogs, which is why I was consulted. Stony's first real bite occurred when he was twelve months old. My investigation of the event told me all I needed to know about this dog's danger factor. At twelve months old, Stony was only a pup when he charged an adult man (who was a friend of Stony's owner and had been around this watch dog several times) who was working on landscaping in the front yard of Stony's home. On one of the many trips this man made to the garage at the back of the house for mulch, Stony (who was hanging out in the back yard with his owner) decided he'd seen enough of this man for one day and deliberately trotted toward him. Stony's owner, noticing this committed behavior, tried repeatedly and forcefully to call his dog back. The newly (self) commissioned watch dog ignored his owner's calls and actually sped as he got closer to the man. When Stony was within striking distance, he jumped up on the unsuspecting friend and bit him just below the shoulder. He bit the man a second time in the arm as the victim tried to defend himself. Stony's owner was right behind him and quickly pulled the aggressor from his friend, but not quickly enough to prevent injury to the innocent outsider.

Again, this was Stony's first biting experience, and what that conveyed to me was extreme confidence, assertiveness, and hostility all rolled into one large, powerful dog. This was not a home visit I looked forward to, but I liked Tom and Doris (no children to worry about in this family thank goodness) and felt for them in their desperate position. They were very fond of their overly zealous body guard who, unfortunately, had become a dangerous menace to the people who lived around them. Both Tom and Doris were absolutely taken aback by Stony's extreme territorial and defensive aggression because they had done their homework before they purchased him. They had visited the breeder to verify she was conscientious and knowledgeable. They were able to spend time with the sire and dam before the litter was whelped. Tom was even able to see a grown pup from a previous breeding. During their research, Tom and Doris didn't come across any kind of hostility that resembled what Stony displayed. I need to mention here that Stony was devoted to his family and had shown no hostility toward them at all. As a whole, Stony was balanced and pleasurable to be around if you were a member of the small group he identified as his family. If you weren't an insider, he saw no sense in taking prisoners. Stony was simply a tough guardian.

When Cathy and I visited Stony, the training challenge that lay ahead was immediately apparent. As we pulled up to the house Tom came out to meet us with Stony on leash, lunging and barking. I'm sure Tom felt somewhat self-conscious over his Tasmanian devil's greeting, and he was therefore reluctant to apply much in the way of control measures. At the same time, he probably felt relieved that help had arrived and he could now turn his big problem over to a professional. Whatever the reason, as I tried to step out of my truck to say hello, Tom allowed Stony to charge right up to within inches of my thighs. Using my door as a shield, I had to repeatedly tell Tom to drag his dog back to a more comfortable distance. All the while, Tom tried to convince Stony that I'm his friend and everything was alright. Stony made it crystal clear through his ongoing hostile display that he didn't care what Tom thought. From Stony's perspective I wasn't his friend, everything was not alright, and Tom definitely was not the captain of their team! So Stony was essentially telling me to get back in my truck, get off HIS property, and don't let the door hit me in the butt on the way out.

I probably don't have to mention this by now, but the first step in bringing Stony's aggressive behavior into check was to put Tom into the position of team leader. By implementing my basic obedience fundamentals, Tom was able to set up new rules of interaction for Stony. I helped Tom create reasonable policies for his watch dog to follow and I showed Tom how to deliver consequences to reinforce these policies. Tom smoothly transformed into the new team captain. Because of the meaningful consequences attached to Tom's new rules of interaction, they naturally trumped Stony's preconceived ideas on how to handle certain situations. Due to this one adjustment in Tom and Stony's relationship, the overly zealous defensiveness that dominated their household took an immediate downturn.

It is important to recall, my obedience fundamentals center on the concepts of canine self control (containing drive and energy), deference to the handler (check with the captain before committing to action), and mindfulness around distractions (clear thinking in the thick of activity). Establishing canine self control responsibilities along with reinforced primary handler policies is the key to aggression control. **The five handling manners (Composure, Food Control, Visitor Control, Open Door Control, and the Walking Exercise) that lead off my basic obedience program are more influential in controlling canine hostility than the five formal commands (Heel, Sit, Down, Stay, and Come) that most people think of as primary control exercises.** All of those control tools are important, but formal directives should take a back seat to good manners. The new relationship we were able to build between Tom and Stony brought the problematic defensiveness into reasonable, supervised control pretty quickly. Stony's territorial aggression was another story.

Tom and Doris' house was situated on a comfortable two acre tract as were the adjacent neighbors on either side of them. Although a tangible barrier did not fence Stony's yard, Tom did have a signal wire fence installed, and had recently erected a spacious exercise pen in the back yard. Unfortunately, neither one of those products did much to protect innocent people from getting bitten in the past. With the signal wire fence, neighbors, delivery persons, and visitors were not physically blocked from walking into Stony's actively guarded territory. Also, with the signal wire fence, Stony's home area appeared visually, at least to him, far reaching and all in compassing. This openness sometimes led Stony to charge through the electric barrier after distant intruders. A heightened, hostile state of behavior would significantly raise Stony's pain threshold. That meant the fence system's electric deterrent (which Stony usually respected) didn't pack enough stopping power to deter him at such aggressive times. In regards to the very nice pen Tom had built, he wasn't in a habit of using it. The entire reason he and Doris bought the two acre home was to afford their dog some freedom to run and exercise. Never imagining owning such an intense watch dog, two acres seemed like a lot of exercise room to Tom and Doris. That's how they ended up in this desperate situation of trying to make Stony fit into their dream. So for all intents and purposes, before I helped Tom restructure the home routine, Stony was in charge of all he could see whenever he was outside.

Getting a grip on Stony's territorial aggression had more to do with what Tom and Doris thought about their current situation than how their dog behaved under the existing conditions. As disheartening as it was for Stony's owners to hear, the first step in the right training direction was redefining their original dream. Owning a friendly canine companion that loved to hang out around the house and enjoyed visiting with outsiders who ventured on to the property wasn't the reality of this situation. So, what they wanted to do had to give way to what they needed to do.

If the plan was to keep Stony, protecting the innocent from injury was the first priority. **In that light, Tom and Doris' view of their family dog as a free spirit had to change. Stony had proven more than a few times in a twelve month period that he could not run loose on his two acre property without abusing the privilege. I do mean privilege, not right.** This privilege needs to be earned by all dogs through acceptable behavior which is determined by the primary handlers and the environmental demands. For instance, a true farm dog might be allowed to run through fifty acres of farm land as long as he doesn't harass the livestock. A condominium dog may only be allowed to run free outside the building if he maintains proximity to his handler and follows basic obedience rules, so as not to interfere with other residents and traffic. A country dog, on the other hand, may be allowed to run over hill and dale as long as he comes home for supper. **The amount of freedom a dog is afforded is better measured by what works than what one wants.**

Along this line of thinking, Stony's situation was analogous to the condominium dog even though he lives in a single dwelling home surrounded by two acres. After presenting the idea of earned freedom, I outlined for Tom and Doris the new outside rules for Stony that absolutely, positively had to be followed no matter what (the exact same rule system I follow at home with my watch dog). **Rule number one: Stony could not be loose outside unless directly supervised by either Tom or Doris (no substitutes for the primary handlers). Rule number two: Whenever supervised outside Stony must** wear a working collar with either a leash, or long line attached. This rule was in effect until Tom and Doris achieved (through the implementation of all ten steps of my basic obedience program) distraction proofed, hands free control. Rule number three: Stony must be secured in his exercise pen with the gate clipped when he was outside without supervision. Rule number four: develop a hush command for Stony (because both Tom and Doris appreciate a little watch dog behavior) like I described in the preceding Defensive section. Rule number five: do not allow physical contact of any kind between Stony and outsiders (even if that means putting Stony in his pen or crate when visitors arrive). Rule number six: assist the signal wire fence (utilizing a leash or long line attached to a working collar) in defining and reinforcing the property lines, especially when distractions are about. Rule number seven: DO NOT CHEAT ON ANY OF THE FIRST SIX RULES.

Since there was no tangible barrier around the property, and because Stony had already proven to be so injurious to outsiders, this was not a training scenario suited for a bark diminishing or remote control collar like we used in Aztec's case. We see a number of clients throughout the year who jump to one of these collars as a quick fix for similar territorial behavior problems. The error with this remedy for territorial situations, like Stony's, is the electric stimulation from the collar is often not an effective enough deterrent to stop the charge of a highly aggressive canine (as was proven by the multiple breeches of the signal wire system Stony was trained on). A tangible barrier or a leash and collar of some kind are necessary to physically ensure the hostile charge will not occur. In addition to this safety concern, conscientious training demands presenting the hostile canine with positive options that are identified by the pleasant consequences connected to them. Diligent instruction can be a challenging task without manageable limitations to the training area.

While Tom and Doris worked with the six outside rules at home, I instructed them on handling manners, formal obedience commands, and defensive aggression control at the training center. Stony wasn't nearly as aggressive away from his home territory, but he was still a far cry from being Mr. Friendly. Stony was still very confident at the center, but not on guard or hostile, further demonstrating how bent he was toward guarding his home area. This approach to Stony's hostile territorial behavior was all consuming for Tom and Doris. They loved that dog though, and were staunchly determined to keep their watch dog happy and outsiders safe.

At the time of this writing it's been several months since Tom and Doris implemented the complete training program for their watch dog. They reported during our last conversation that there have been no successful bites (two attempts that were thwarted because of handler preparedness) on Stony's part. Tom also said that it took him and Doris a couple of months to comfortably adjust to the new outside routines and handling rules. But now that they've adjusted, Tom couldn't imagine going back to the old way (unsupervised freedom outside) of doing things, even with their next dog who will hopefully lean more toward the affable dog of their dreams.

Chapter Seven

Protest Aggression

Like the previous chapters on defensiveness and territory guarding, the hostile considerations associated with protest and intolerance are very similar but not necessarily overlapping. I've identified aggression types (by the trigger that sets that explosive wheel into motion) for the sole purpose of efficient handling at my training center. I do believe that labeling the type of hostility greatly aids even a novice handler to focus on the cause, effect, and consequences of the dog-in-training's behavioral issues. Since focus is a main ingredient in proficient aggression management, the effort of labeling is worth the while. The main difference between a protest and an intolerance reaction is that with protest a handler is met with a degree of aggressive refusal when trying to get his canine student to follow a directive or respond to some kind of instruction. Many times with an assertive, independent, serious dog, the catalyst for his hostile resistance is not so much the degree of the challenge he's been asked to face but the act of acquiescing itself. Volition is a valued treasure for a strong-willed, confident dog.

Last year I had a canine student that exhibited pure protest and disturbance hostility with no aggressive display in any other situation. When giving instruction to others, I often refer to this dog and her training because the triggers that set off her hostility, her reactions to the environment and handling, along with the training procedure employed to manage her behavior were all so universally classic. Her name was Rouge. She was a vocal, happy, Red Bone coon hound dressed in the traditional mahogany coat. She was approaching young adulthood when her comical griping and complaining became more serious. Within the first week of coming home from the breeder, Larry (her owner and a repeat client) remembers Rouge vocalizing disagreement over many things such as being picked up if it wasn't her idea, or moving her on the couch when she was sleepy, or simply attempting to put a collar on her. He remembered in those early days thinking she was funny and would probably grow out of it, especially with conscientious handling. A decade earlier, Larry had gone through our full basic obedience course with another hound that didn't express any of this behavior. So for Larry, even though he was an experienced handler, when it came to Rouge he was navigating through uncharted waters. If Larry's previous instruction did nothing else, it prompted him to take early action in dealing with Rouge's rapidly intensifying hostility.

When Larry first brought Rouge into the training center I remember her shining like a new penny, practically grinning from long ear to long ear with the excitement of anticipation. Before I had a chance to say hello, Larry forewarned me, "Don't let her good looks and happy face fool you, she's nothing like my last hound. I believe this little witch would bite if pushed far enough." By push, Larry meant ordinary, everyday handling and maintenance just like he expected from his previous dog. Rouge definitely possessed the demeanor to fool a person because she was a little different than the average protesting dog. For the most part she was lighthearted and bubbly rather than a bit sour or grouchy, so her hostile complaints tended to catch the family by surprise.

Coming through the front door, I could tell Larry had already been working with his new companion. We were able to shake hands and greet each other while Rouge almost sat quietly on a tolerably taught leash. Getting Rouge to respond to formal commands really wasn't Larry's concern at the moment. He was confident that he had acquired enough experience training his last companion to teach his new student formal directives. I was tempted to cut directly to the chase with this situation; I wanted to put Rouge in a crate or change out her collar in order to witness her Jekyll to Hyde transformation myself. But more than anyone else, I knew successful management of dog aggression had to begin with the development of canine self control through handling manners. That approach cannot be stressed enough! I did not want Larry to demonstrate his difficulties with Rouge in regards to her protest, which would potentially set up another victory for the dog at the expense of the handler. **Here is a good rule of thumb to operate by when trying to manage hostile canine behavior: skirt around aggressive conflict with the dog-in-training until the canine's conduct can be properly addressed within a structured training environment.**

My intention with Rouge was to run her through all five of the handling manners exercises (in order) on her first two visits, so by the third lesson (which occurred about three weeks after lesson one) we could tackle her aggressive behavior head on. The first exercise, composure (maintain proximity to handler without bothering anyone in any way), proved to be somewhat challenging for the Redbone. Without the help of directives, restraints, and reprimands (which Larry utilized instead of fomenting self control in his coon hound), Rouge found it very difficult to curb her pushiness and refrain from forcing engagement with those around her. We could start building tolerance and handler deference (in other words, self control) right here, without the hassle of hostility.

Think of composure as the footing for the manners foundation that the house of control rests upon. When Larry pointed to the hostile, structural flaw in the house of control that he and Rouge lived in, it never occurred to him to look beyond the superficial cracks. Like an engineer, my job was to assist Larry in an investigation as to the cause of the cracks, given the limitations of the building material (a robust Redbone coon hound) and environmental conditions (household schedules and family arrangements). It's likely that a conscientious engineer will start at the bottom of the troubled structure and work his investigation upward, so as not to miss any possible cause (imagining a domino effect) for the structural cracks. In Larry's defense, history and experience with troubled structures (relationships) quickly sends an engineer (dog trainer) to the footing and foundation (composure and manners) for clues to solving a problem. Rouge was a bright student, and once Larry connected meaningful consequences to the decisions she made in regards to the new policies that were created, Rouge accepted her responsibilities more readily than we anticipated. At the beginning of his instruction, Larry had a difficult time letting go of emotional reprimands and militant commands as controlling maneuvers. Undoubtedly, the most poignant message manners instruction impresses upon novice dog trainers is "lighten up" let the dog learn naturally. Allow the dog to make a decision, and consistently supply the timely appropriate consequence. Sometimes doing less really is doing more!

By his own admission, Larry believed Rouge was smarter than his last companion, and that meant he needed to get over the surprise of her trying to manipulate their relationship. Testing the parameters of a rule is a direct route to understanding the intricacies of the rule. The smarter the canine student is, the more testing there may be which may create better understanding. Don't automatically view a new dog pushing the envelope as a bad thing.

After a brief period of concentration, supplying (emotion free) leash and collar tugs whenever Rouge bothered anyone or attempted to leave the handler's area, redirected her focus. Supplying genuine reward (physical and verbal praise or food bonus) for effort in the desired direction, Larry ultimately reached hands free, command free, casual control over Rouge. I had Larry mentally mark this pivotal moment in his relationship with Rouge. Instruction in composure (the first of the five handling manners) was bringing about energy and drive control, handler deference, and mindfulness around distractions that was missing in Rouge. Simultaneously, a respectful relationship was being cultivated between the dog and the primary handler.

At the training center, we typically include grooming control as part of the composure exercise. Learning how to passively accept handler manipulation is an important concept for any companion dog to understand. Given Rouge's case, I knew in advance that she had a real issue with putting on a collar. Therefore, it was likely that we were going to run into assertive resistance when brushing her head, cleaning ears, or checking her teeth. My initial training plan when trying to mitigate aggressive protest or resistance is to work close to, but around, the specific volatile issue until I feel I've achieved maximum, positive control over the canine student in every other way. Therefore, when Larry and I worked on grooming Rouge, we concentrated on having her stand absolutely still (short, loose leash in hand but no restraint) while we brushed her body and clipped her nails. We purposely left her head alone until we gained better overall control in the days ahead. Besides, we had plenty on our plate simply getting Rouge to hold a stand and resist wrestling when the brush touched her body.

The second exercise, food control (eat only from the hand of a primary handler or from the assigned feeding dish), provides an excellent opportunity to clarify a critical aspect in the human-dog relationship. The point we want to drive home to the dog is turn down what you want and always defer to your handler. When a dog abides by this rule, the message he sends to his primary handler is, "You're more important than I am!" Although Rouge has a voracious appetite, politeness around food and meal time etiquette was easy for her to accept. Politeness with food also means taking treats from the hand in a gentile fashion, and we started working on that with Rouge in the first sixty seconds of her instruction. She had developed a habit of taking fingers with the treat, so by the time we officially moved to the food control exercise Rouge was already moving in a mannerly direction. As a reminder, the details of how to develop the handling manners can be found in my first book, "The Ten Natural Steps to Training the Family Dog."

The third exercise, visitor control (do not initiate contact with the visitor, wait for the visitor to engage, and avoid placing teeth or feet on the visitor), translated into hysteria management for Rogue. I think it's very important to begin this visitor control exercise from the seated position. A utilitarian type of chair is required for freedom of handling. Fixing dog and handler to a specific location limits wrestling and dancing with the dog learning self control (without restraint, commands or bribes). Self restraint will be the very tool that keeps the canine student's feet and teeth off of the visitor no matter how the visitor behaves.

Keeping in mind that all living beings outside the immediate family can be defined as visitors, the first challenge I set up for Larry and Rouge was a boisterous man walking a playful pup. As soon as the man and his pup entered in the training room, Rouge became overly excited over the bouncing youngster. Larry had his hands full reinforcing the loose leash and "don't bother anyone" rule. It's just the exercise he needed to thoroughly impress Rouge with his improved handling techniques. Not one time did Larry bark out a command or emotionally reprimand the Redbone. He insisted on a loose leash and she gave it to him. Larry's leash and collar corrections were crisp and potent every time Rouge tried to shake off any of the new policies. If Larry had been any milder, his powerful hound would have easily discounted his attempts to reinforce the rules, and the struggle for team captain would rage on. Even though this was only his second dog to take through training, Larry's praise and rewards for Rouge's good efforts were spot on. Only with the subtlest of good behaviors did I have to encourage Larry to pay up with a positive consequence. Because of Larry's extraordinary handling ability, we were able to utilize multiple visitors simultaneously with Rouge's leash on the ground, while he and I idled about the training area engaging visitors at will. The young Redbone had never worked so hard in her life. What a trooper Rouge turned out to be by gravitating next to Larry and accepting interaction from humans and dogs without overreacting. All of this control existed without commands, restraints, or bribes. I think with this exercise more than any other, Rouge began to look at her handler differently. I think for the first time in their relationship the young Redbone looked to Larry for leadership.

The fourth exercise was door control (wait for the primary handler's permission to cross a newly exposed threshold). I combined this with exercise number five, walking instruction (travel left of the handler's center line while maintaining a full loose leash). Since Larry had already established with Rouge some semblance of heeling, I felt jumping into walk from the open doorway would not be terribly taxing for the two. By the relieved expression on Rouge's face when we directed her attention away from the visitors and onto the door, I felt sure the last two exercises wouldn't be as trying as the previous one. Standing before a newly opened doorway holding your dog on six feet of loose leash, is one of the surest signs that you call the shots. Right away, I kicked this exercise up a couple of notches for this pair because they did have a little head start in obedience, and both Larry and Rouge seemed to take to training so readily. So as soon as we were able to convey to Rouge that holding at the doorway was her responsibility, I had Larry step back and forth across the threshold while his companion patiently watched and waited. Dropping the leash and repeating the exercise was the next step. With this second round of crossing the threshold, I encouraged

Larry to cover more ground. Before Rouge even had the first opportunity to cross the threshold with Larry's permission, I had multiple dog walkers pass by her going in and out the doorway. Success with this kind of open door challenge meant Rouge was primed and ready to take her newly acquired self control skills on the road.

The task of proper walking for a dog boils down to three separate duties, following and yielding while maintaining a loose leash. Think of walking as a relaxed version of heeling, which is essentially a neck to leg position a dog is responsible for when under that command. With the casual walking exercise, I want the dog to have some liberties. That's why we usually afford the canine student six feet of leash for this task. The real challenge for the student is appreciating the six feet of freedom while abiding by the loose leash and left of the handler's center line rules. Once mastered, however, dog and handler can travel unlimited distances while maintaining this comfortable relationship. Proper heeling, on the other hand, is far too demanding and rigid for a dog and handler to keep up for any real distance. Therefore, I've always found it best to develop a solid walking exercise before attempting to teach heel. Besides, walking is where the rubber meets the road. If a dog-in-training is capable of enjoying the scenery while bouncing around on a full loose leash, somewhere left of the handler's center line while being able to speed up, slow down, and change direction to accommodate his handler, he has honed his skills of commitment to the team leader. This was the very thing Larry needed Rouge to do before he could expect her to let go of protesting. So out the door we went!

The first series of walking maneuvers for Larry involved multiple right-about turns in an attempt to slow Rouge down. When her feet hit the grass and she felt the loose leash, she was gone! The last thing on her mind was Larry. Adhering to our strategy, each time Rouge bolted, Larry would turn one hundred and eighty degrees and charge in the opposite direction. Keeping his momentum up and a secure grip on the leash handle, Larry would spin Rouge each time she ran in front to set pace and direction. Larry was making a bold statement by his quiet maneuvers, since leading and following are mutually exclusive pursuits when it comes to team work. Each time Rouge chose to lead, Larry thwarted her effort and immediately returned the loose leash without command or reprimand. Rogue was free to choose again. Part of the proper mindset of a good handler is not to show emotional upset no matter which course of action a dog may choose. Larry conducted himself beautifully through this exercise like he had done throughout this first lesson. He refrained (as challenging as it was) from barking out commands, he kept his negative feelings to himself and he delivered soothing reward or impressive leash deterrents the moment they were needed. It took several attempts, but Rouge finally came to the conclusion that following Larry would be more productive than trying to lead Larry.

Now that Rouge was content to follow her team leader, it was time to impart one more bit of walking wisdom. Yield or give way when the team captain comes left-about in direction. This idea is best conveyed when handler and dog are walking along a barrier like a fence line or the side of a building. The barrier should run along the dog's left side with no more than about twelve inches between the barrier and the dog's left side. Our intent and purpose with this maneuver is to force the dog into reverse gear to exaggerate the yielding to the handler concept. Utilizing a barrier prevents the canine student from swinging out away from the handler when the left-about turn begins, thereby forestalling any attempt on the dog's part to convert this yield and turn exercise into a dance. I had Larry slowly walk with Rouge along the unobstructed side of my training center. With Rouge about a foot and a half away from the building, I instructed Larry to turn left-about with a slow and steady pace. His objective was to scuff, bump and leash tug his way into Rouge until she fell back to the comfort of the general left of center line position, once again following in the proper direction at the desired pace. We repeated this process over and over again, mixing in the open yard and right about turns until Rouge was focused on Larry and where he was going. Larry actually laughed out loud through much of the walking exercise, being stimulated by the competition over who would be team leader. He was also amazed to experience how determined his young hound was to be in charge. As a side note, it makes for far better training to view your strong minded dog's competitive spirit as amusing rather than frustrating.

These last two exercises solidified three key points of Larry and Rouge's new relationship. The first point is that Larry is the team leader because he establishes policies and supplies consequences. The second point, Rouge is responsible for controlling her drive and energy and she needs to defer to Larry before launching into action. The third point, distractions do not alter the relationship rules. By legitimizing these new guidelines we were able to make Larry the most important being in Rouge's life, and we accomplished this through handling manners instruction without hostile confrontation. The sequence of manners before aggression control meant Larry would have a substantial leadership edge when it came time to tackle those sticky hostile situations.

Larry was eager, of course, to get on top of Rouge's hostility behavior. He was also an experienced, coon hound handler. So after just two, one hour lessons devoted entirely to manners along with two practice periods of about two weeks each, Larry and Rouge were well on their way to a new relationship without yet having to butt heads over aggression issues. **I cannot stress enough how invaluable instruction in manners is in preparation for hostile behavior management.** Although Larry was eager, he was not sloppy. His diligent training throughout Rouge's self control instruction returned high dividends from the moment we began addressing her protesting issues.

By lesson number three, I was more than satisfied with Larry's overall position as team captain, and I was genuinely impressed with Rouge's level of self control (hands free, in the thick of distraction). It was finally time to cut to the chase. I chose to begin aggression management with Rouge's resistance to enter her crate when told. Larry desperately needed the crate to limit Rouge's destructive behavior while he was at work, and to finish her house breaking. I do want to mention here that the best time to begin crate conditioning is the first day the pup or adult dog is brought into the home. Conditioning for any kind of confinement should start with a positive spin. For example, meals can be served in the confinement area creating a strong pleasant impression. Using the confinement area as a partial playground with retrieving games is an easy way to improve a crate or pen's appeal. At the very least, confinement should be introduced to a new canine in a pleasurable fashion with the use of treats, toys, and agreeable handling. When Larry initially brought Rouge into his home as a puppy, he tried some positive crate conditioning but he quickly gave into her complaining which set up the stronger resistance he's now facing.

Hoping for the best but always having to prepare for the worst, I placed a large sturdy crate in one of our training rooms and cleared away all objects around it to make sure we would have ample training space. I pushed the crate's back end up against the wall to minimize it sliding around. I also left the crate door open to facilitate a smooth approach and entry. Like always, before attempting to deal with any kind of canine hostility, I made sure Rouge was wearing a secure leash and slip, training collar. In previous lessons I cautioned Larry about wearing the appropriate shoes and clothing when he worked with his strong, athletic hound. This is an important consideration anytime someone steps into the role of a dog handler. However, when a handler is faced with the task of training an aggressive canine student, the proper attire can be the difference between effective results and clumsy (possibly injurious) failure.

The uniform that we wear at the training center is not simply for looks. As dog trainers, we need to be able to move our upper and lower body freely while maintaining solid contact with the ground. It is easy for an athletic, middle size dog (and up) to knock us off balance or wrap us up in our own leash. Keep in mind when our canine companion knocks us down or back, when the dog calls a halt to the training process, or when the student redirects a handler's intended plan, the dog is in control AND HE KNOWS IT! The stakes are all that much higher when we're dealing with a potentially aggressive dog. So in Rouge's case, I wanted everything to be as secure as possible, so Larry would be able to remain calmly on task with only minimal (I would like to say no risk but that's not realistic) risk of injury or retreat.

Larry's recipe for success would be a proper mindset along with a well thought out strategy of how to overcome Rouge's hostile crating resistance. A proper mindset was the positive image of the finished product. At this stage of training, I wanted Larry to visualize calmly walking Rouge up to her crate and giving her a pleasant command to enter. After a one second response time, swiftly and safely put her in. Like a pole vaulting athlete preparing for his event, a conscientious dog trainer should mentally walk through the sequence of steps that lead to success before there is any attempt to handle the dog. Prior to executing his plan, Larry had to mentally work out how to handle a snafu that a pole vaulter never has to contend with, aggressive resistance from his pole (Rouge)!

The strategy that Larry and I discussed in preparation for the training success was detailed and specific. Larry should walk slowly and directly toward the open gate of the crate with Rouge on a short (about fifteen inches) loose leash (held firmly in two hands) in the traditional left hand position. Upon reaching the door of the crate give her one pleasant command to enter. If she enters, lavish her with rewards. If she refuses to load after a one second response time, remain focused on the front of the crate while applying leash tension with one or two hands toward the crate opening, while at the same time pushing her rear end with a hand or leg toward the opening. Allow for no emotional reaction in response to Rouge's resistance (hold on to a business like attitude). There should be no dancing, retreating, or circling for a re-approach if at all possible. If Rouge were to force Larry into retreat or a re-approach, Larry would need to prepare for a stronger battle on the second attempt because his dog registered a victory over the previous struggle and now believes she may win the war! After failure to enter the crate, move to an extended leash correction (as I've described in the Chapter on Management) the instant resistance becomes hostile and directed toward the handler. Do not dance or give ground during the extended correction and keep all the action in the appropriate theater of training, which is the small area in front of the crate. The moment Rouge's aggression has quelled as a consequence of the extended correction, release the upward leash tension allowing her front feet to once again rest on the floor and instantly return to the task of placing her in the crate (no pausing for recovery after the extended correction will be necessary). Once Rouge has entered the crate, close the gate leaving the leash attached to her collar and extending over the top of the gate. If Rouge remains quiet in her crate for a few moments, soothing praise is in order. If Rouge is rowdy or restless in the crate once the gate is closed, ignore her until she calms and then supply soothing praise. If Rouge is hostile toward the handler after the gate has been closed, apply an extended correction by pulling the leash taut through the crate door until she calms (about ten seconds or so), and after she remains calm for a short period, give her soothing praise.

With the strategy laid out and a clear image of success on Larry's mind, Larry made his first attempt at putting Rouge in the crate. Before Larry was half way to the crate, I had to disrupt his concentrated effort with my most prolific advice, "SLOW DOWN!" **It's natural for all of us to hurry through a dreaded, unpleasant experience. By working through a potentially unpleasant exercise slowly and calmly, we can help mitigate a dog's anxiety. If a slow pace is established, both handler and dog are given time to think clearly.** A slower pace allows for concise handling, and at the same time sends a message to the canine student that everything is alright. Rouge put on the brakes about two body lengths before reaching the gate opening, and Larry had to finish the approach by dragging her forward into the loose leash, walking position. With Rouge as stiff as a statue, Larry points to the gate opening and pleasantly says to her one time, "Crate."

After one long moment passed, Rouge was still stiff as a statue staring directly at Larry purposefully avoiding the confinement idea. Here I told Larry not to forget our strategy, a nice long moment to respond had passed and Rouge made her decision to not enter the crate. It was now time to use leash tension and tail pushing to get Larry's strong willed hound into the crate. As soon as Larry leaned forward to apply leash tension, Rouge exploded into an aggressive fit, raring up on her hind legs and biting at the leash and Larry's hands. With the reflexes of a young man (which he was not), Larry moved to an extended correction that was made possible by the shortened leash (part of our strategy) and firm two hand grip. Rouge's hostile tantrum was short lived because of the poor floor purchase and the overall feeling of powerlessness that the extended correction brought about. This handling technique also better protected Larry from being bitten, and it kept Rouge from flailing around and hurting herself. A properly executed extended correction can minimize the risk of injury to handler and dog.

Once Rouge proved to be genuinely calm, Larry relaxed the leash extension and repeated "Crate." This time Rouge went into hard reverse almost jolting Larry to the ground, but he held his ground and eventually pulled his fit-throwing Redbone by into the left hand walk position. By now both handler and dog were winded but Larry was so close to success I had to encourage him not to let up. I said, "Tell her again." Larry never once lost his cool and on this third attempt Rouge refused to crate again. With this third refusal, however, she didn't rear up and try to bite or try to pull Larry out of the room. Rogue tried yet another ploy by remaining planted to the ground. With some prompting from me, Larry went into action using leash tension toward the gate opening with a hand pushing her rump. This time he managed to physically put Rouge into the crate. It was time to close the gate, pause, and recover for just a bit while Rouge reluctantly relaxed in the crate. For Larry, the greatest challenge had been met. This was Rouge's the first successful placement in the crate despite her defiant storms. This was not the time for a delay in training though, Larry and Rouge needed to end this exercise on a more positive note. So after a little soothing praise for settling into her confinement, Larry opened the crate door and told Rouge to walk. The Redbone shot out of her crate with such enthusiasm that she almost knocked Larry over. Her tail was wagging and her face was smiling though like there had never been a battle of wills.

Rouge's "no big deal" reaction to her thwarted protest is more common than not. Every dog owner should bear in mind that a canine's willingness to move past struggles is directly proportional to the trainer's even temperament and fair hand. After Larry spent a few moments petting his wiggling hound, I had him walk around the training room a few times to finish clearing the air of any lingering negativity. A little bit of pleasant interaction with a few rounds of casual walking went a long way in establishing an upbeat tempo for the next round. After three trips around the room, Larry headed straight for the crate. This time he was packing more confidence, not only from getting his strong Redbone in the crate but also from managing her hostility without anyone being injured.

Rouge could definitely feel the change in the wind this time around, as signaled by her not so high and cocky tail carriage. She still wanted to hold back from the crate, but Larry was faster at pulling her forward. Sitting quietly and not so stiffly at Larry's side, Rouge was somewhat avoiding the crate. Just like the first attempt, Larry pointed at the gate opening and said "Crate." A full one second response time came and went, and there sat the coon hound, waiting to see what might happen with this refusal. Truthfully, Rouge was out of options. She tried every form of resistance that worked for her in the past to no avail. Ultimately, she still wound up in the crate. This time the willful Redbone was hoping Larry might fall back into his old behavior pattern and try to coax and plead with her. **Even a little slip back into old methods here would have been disastrous for the training program. Any little chink in Larry's armor would have been all Rouge needed to bolster her confidence for another round of resistance.**

Once again I prodded Larry, "Move and demonstrate your resolve". Larry again applied leash tension, keeping his head back in preparation for the hostile explosion he felt was coming. The Redbone dug in but didn't explode. Larry had two hands on the leash to combat Rouge's strength, so he used his leg to assist in a pushing her rear end. After a couple of moments of stalemate, Rouge charged into the crate as if to say "Let's get it over with!" Although Rouge was not "fully cooperative" on this last exercise, her resistance was neither violent nor long lived. This was Tangible proof that we were on the right track.

Protest Aggression

Once the head is tucked and the leash is taut, try to keep the reluctant student moving

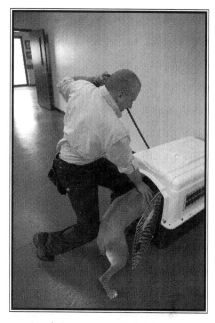

Don't forget to assist with your leg by pushing the tail end

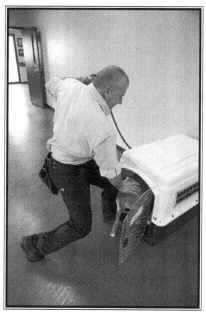

Don't let up until the entire dog is inside the crate

Early in the training process, an observant handler should be watchful for even the slightest sign of progress or improvement in their dog's behavior. Verification that a training program is headed in the right direction is not optional, it's essential. Without early verification that a path of instruction is effective, I typically call a halt to training and reevaluate the entire situation. With some aggressive cases, I will slow the initial training pace down to allow a dog more time to completely assimilate and accept his new responsibilities. In other cases I may increase the pace of training to keep the canine student challenged and engaged. Adjustments in distraction levels (up or down) are often necessary throughout a dog's training career.

The dog training process, as a whole, should be viewed as a malleable progression. A flexible instruction program affords the necessary adjustments to accurately match unlimited variations of training challenges that any given student can bring to the training table. In regards to Rouge's instruction, had her hostility increased with each attempt to place her in the crate despite Larry's applicable handling, I would have aborted further attempts to place her in the modest size crate in favor of using an oversize cage for ease of execution. In a case like this one, I may have had Larry and Rouge revisit the self control exercises for a few more weeks with increased distractions to forge better handler deference and drive control. Sometimes all a handler can do to minimize loss in leadership status is execute manageable obedience exercises within the immediate proximity of the trouble spot (the crate in this instance). This training strategy will gradually wear down a student's desire to resist, while at the same time reduce the potency of a negative idea through exposure or familiarity. The bottom line is don't be afraid to deviate from a well thought out training plan if no improvement in the dog's behavior is witnessed after a concentrated effort.

I could feel Larry wearing down with Rouge's last resistance effort. So we left her in the crate just long enough to close the gate, verbally sooth her, and offer some food reward which she gladly accepted. Since Larry's defiant coon hound readily consumed her treats, Rouge again demonstrated the whole defiance game she initiated was not really that upsetting to her. Unfortunately, the team captain didn't share her sentiment. Although Larry was beginning to drag a bit, as soon as the Redbone swallowed our offerings I had him whisk her out of confinement for another walking trip around the room (to clear the emotional air).We then headed right back to the crate. (Capitalizing on momentum is a key component in managing a strong willed animal. Like most pursuits in this world, it takes much less energy to keep a big boulder rolling than it does to repeatedly let it stop and restart the process.) As Larry lined up with the open crate for his next attempt (about three dog lengths away), Rouge bolted toward the opening trying to drag her handler and into the little condo. One might think at this point, "Success at last". However, as I explained to Larry, if we allowed Rouge to break loose leash and walking rules in order to load up in a crate then we are, in essence, conveying to the canine student that she is still (at least partially) calling the shots. Condoning her unacceptable bolting and dragging behavior leaves the door of defiance open for future battles. Also, by permitting his Redbone to successfully charge into the crate, Larry would have been (albeit innocently) fostering the unnaturally, strong emotions Rouge has attached to this normally benign event. Our plan from the outset of training has been to reduce the influence Rouge has over her relationship with Larry, and reduce or eliminate the intensity and frequency of her emotional upsurges. For these two reasons, it was crucial in his pursuit of aggression management that Larry took control of Rouge and require her to walk as she was taught and load into the crate on command.

The coonhound really caught her handler off guard with the explosion of energy, and I had to quickly jump in front of the crate to keep her from making entry. Larry wanted to let Rouge enter the crate so he could call it a victory and call it a day. But Larry hired me to help bring his dog's hostility into control, not simply put it off to another day, so I insisted he make yet another attempt. Larry had the jump on his dog this time, so when he saw Rouge visually lock onto the crate he did a quick, right-about turn to regain her focus just like he had been doing with walking practice. By bringing her focus around to him rather than on the crate, Larry was able to get Rouge within about a body length of the gate opening where he had her sit for a second before telling her "Crate". Close enough! This time I agreed, we could call the training experience a success. After a long battle of wills, it's nice for everyone to have time to disengage, and for Rouge this meant relaxing in her newly appreciated private space. It took about fifteen minutes for me to summarize the entire training event with Larry. As soon as we finished, I encouraged him to release Rouge from the crate and spend some quality time playing with her. There is no better way to get a dog to shed negative energy than with positive, physical exertion.

Now that Larry had surmounted the largest aggressive obstacle between him and his Redbone, during the fourth lesson I intended to tackle the rest of their snags. Rouge's remaining protest issues seemed to center on head sensitivity and feelings of vulnerability when her head was restrained (e.g. slipping collars on and off, cleaning ears, inspecting teeth, et cetera). These are relatively common sensitivities in the theater of protest. A very challenging aspect of this kind of protest is having our easily to damaged hands operating so close to the dogs powerful, lightening fast jaws. I would like to tell you that there is a clever way around this conundrum, but in reality we only have concentrated focus and adroit leash operation. An innocent owner may ask why we don't muzzle their dog to work on these risky problems? Not to overstate the obvious, but to Rouge, muzzling would be one of the more offensive moves a handler could make. The truth is, if we could put a muzzle on her, there wouldn't be much of a problem to work on anyway.

I was fortunate in this case that Larry had wrestled a slip collar on Rouge some weeks ago (the last time she actually bit him), and he left it on so he wouldn't have to fight with her every day. I think that was a smart plan, and since it was a quality working collar there was no need to change it out for another one. This meant Rouge's actual training with me began with the pleasant, manageable exercises of handling manners and formal commands. I did not have Larry legitimately address Rouge's hostility until he had developed some handling skills and I decided when she was ready for crate conditioning. Sometimes I don't have this opportunity for a positive start because I have to get a secure collar on a dog before any training can begin. If the new student wants no part of the collar, I'm faced with a problem for my first exercise (the problem Larry addressed weeks prior to training).

A slip collar is such a magical piece of equipment with its hostility diffusing capabilities (through extended corrections), I can't imagine working on aggression control without it. I tell the owners of hostile dogs that the slip collar and leash are the best form of bite protection. So usually the first task on the training agenda is getting a high-quality collar on the prospective student. Always think of introducing your dog to equipment as a conditioning process. As best you can for as long as you can, build an association between the equipment and something genuinely positive (for a defiant dog this usually means something more than just praise). My mainstay for positive associations is food. If a dog has an appetite, you can't beat food as a motivator. Associating the training collar with a daily walk or play time is also a solid plan. When you bring out the leash and collar (or muzzle, harness, nail clippers, or crate for that matter), bring on the good stuff.

Let's say you're in Larry's position and you did your best to make putting on the collar a positive experience, but your dog still strongly resists. Now what? Here's what we do at the training center. Make a noose of your leash by putting the snap through the handle and sliding the handle down the leash until you have a loop much larger than your dog's head. Utilizing positive association, calmly and discretely slip the leash loop over the canine student's head. The snap end of the leash will now act as the handle end. The loop should be tightened until it's comfortably snug, making sure the dog cannot forcefully remove his head but that he has free airflow. From this point, the dog can be handled almost as well as if he were wearing a slip collar. Before I begin any instructive handling, though, I want to place an oversize slip collar on the student. If I'm working with a formidable dog like Rouge, I may select a collar two, or three, sizes too big to begin with. I want placement over the head to be quick and easy, but the collar can't be so large as not to function (fast closing and opening action).

With a little shopping around, you should be able to find slip collars that have a toggle at one end rather than a ring. This allows for a connection around the dog's neck without having to slide the collar over the head. One of the down sides to this type of collar is without the leash attached, it's possible for the toggle to incidentally pass through the floating ring and fall off when the dog shakes or wrestles around. In Rouge's case, Larry couldn't put any type of collar on her without a battle, so the toggle collar wouldn't have helped him much. Regardless of how ugly the first noose or collar sessions are, don't let up with the positive conditioning or practice. Placing collars on and off should be part of every dog's daily life. It's often prudent to begin and end the collar conditioning session using the leash as a noose. A handler may do this for as many training sessions as it takes to reach a dependable comfort and safety level.

For Larry, lesson number four was a revisit to the grooming control exercises that we partially covered at the onset of his instruction. On this revisit however, we centered our effort on handling Rouge's head rather than avoiding it like we did in the beginning. By this point in training, Larry had been practicing the grooming exercise for weeks (everything but head manipulation). Rouge was accustomed to being placed in a stand and holding still while having her body brushed and toweled. So this is where lesson four began, with the easy and familiar. I wanted Larry to make sure he set Rouge up for an early reward just like we did with the crate training. **An easy and positive beginning to an aggression control session should be the standard approach. We also desire a positive finish where success and reward leave lasting impressions. This approach to hostile control work helps immeasurably in the digestion of the sometimes not so pleasant central portion of training.**

To facilitate quick action, I had Larry holding the short, loose leash in his left hand. The brush was in his right hand as he began brushing Rouge's neck and working up towards her head. As soon as the brush reached the point between her ears, Rouge turned to snap at the brush. Larry, being well practiced now, instantly applied a short extended correction (a tight leash and collar for only several seconds with Rouge's front feet remaining on the ground) using his left hand only. The purpose of the extended correction was to tighten the leash at a forty-five degree angle up and forward to lock Rouge's head in place. This allowed Larry to safely hold her body in place while continuing to brush her with his right hand. It was very important at this moment in training that the brushing of her head continued while her body was held virtually still and properly positioned. If the brushing of the head had been aborted even briefly, Rouge's aggressive action toward the brush would have been rewarded by the delay. By the same token, if Larry would have retreated with the brush to another easier part of Rouge's body, she would have registered this as a victory also. The thrust of our training exercise was to clearly demonstrate to Rouge that she could no longer give orders as the team captain, and from now on, Larry was not going to back away from her head because she insisted on it.

Anyone managing a similar hostile situation when grooming or manipulating a dog should keep in mind, early in training we're not interested in thorough brushing, nail clipping or ear cleaning. Our concentration is on behavior shaping and moving the student ever closer to safe and appropriate conduct. Thorough grooming and meticulous collar adjustment will come later when the dog's improved behavior allows for it. Like a piece of pottery, no matter how eager you are to finish a vase with glaze, you must be patient and thoroughly prepare the clay or else you'll end up with a failed project instead of a beautiful product.

Because Larry had weeks of diligent training preceding this exercise, Rouge's aggressive protest was only half hearted, and the risk of injury to the handler and dog had been greatly reduced. With only a couple of short extended corrections, Larry was able to lightly brush Rouge's face, lift her ears, and adjust her collar. Though the strong minded Redbone didn't like the grooming any more now than she did earlier in their relationship, she was simply more tolerant and more willing to defer to her team leader. Larry couldn't have asked any more from her at this stage of training, which is why I encouraged Larry to give her a few well received treats along with some soothing praise. So even though Rouge was still not a star grooming student, she was at least manageable and behaviorally speaking, moving in the right direction. After several rounds of grooming (pushing Rouge's tolerance a little further each time) that were separated by stimulating periods of play and obedience exercises, we ended with a very successful, and positive, lesson four.

I didn't need to see Larry and Rouge again. They were on a fast track to a balanced relationship, so they finished up their training at home. We did have one long phone consultation about muzzle conditioning for Rouge. If any breed of dog at any age gives even a small indication that aggressive behavior may play a part in his handling response, don't delay with muzzle preparations. In Rouge's case, after nearly a year of hostile practice, muzzle preparation took weeks. With early recognition of aggressive potential, a dog can be conditioned to a muzzle in only days so that it becomes as familiar to the dog as his leash and collar. Forget about any stigma associated with this piece of equipment. That negative feeling stems from misunderstanding and gets in the way of utilizing an effective tool. Looking down on muzzles and their restrictiveness is comparable to looking down on car seats and their restrictiveness. The main purpose of a muzzle or a car seat is safety, and no one can deny they work!

Chapter Eight

Intolerance Aggression

"I'm resting on the couch, don't sit so close!" "I'm trying to see who's coming in the door, quit pushing past me!" "I'm not in the mood for affection, stop petting me!" All of these canine reactions can be expressed as hostile complaints, resembling Rouge's aggressive protest to Larry's handling. The significant difference between intolerance and protest though, is that with intolerance no legitimate handling or directive is needed to evoke the canine's belligerence. In the vast majority of intolerance aggression cases we work on at the training center, all that's needed to trigger the canine family member's hostility is casual, incidental interaction. That light trigger makes this kind of aggression more difficult to avoid or work around and sometimes harder to anticipate. Aggressive protest and intolerance aggression are separated by a distinct difference in their triggers and they therefore require a slightly different training plan. Remember, the sole purpose of distinguishing the aggressive categories in the first place, is to achieve training efficiency. Categorizing the various types of hostile expression according to the triggers that elicit the unwanted behavior, greatly aids in the development of canine training plans and pinpoint handler instruction.

"Grumpy" or "grouchy" could describe the average canine that comes into the training center as an intolerance aggression case; however that isn't fare or entirely accurate. A better description may be selectively intolerant. That's why this type of hostility can be so perplexing to owners. A common question we field at the training center from owners of low tolerance dogs is "What did I do wrong?" "I was just petting him and he started growling." "I was trying to get him to curl up on my lap and he snapped at me!" "I guess I bumped into him as I was squeezing out the door and he nipped my leg!" Normally, by the time I meet the intolerant dog and his owners, most members of the family have run into the assertive canine's wrath one way or another. When I ask the family with an intolerant canine for their top item on the training wish list; it's not unusual for them to request a change in temperament or personality rather than a change in behavior.

It's of the utmost importance to understand the difference between altering a facet of character and shaping a behavioral response. The hope for even a small change in personality is going to be more than what training can deliver. With diligent instruction I can convince a defensive canine that the team captain is in control, so stand down from the job you love and relax while the outsider comes and goes. With consistent handling I can remove the reward or thrill from a dog aggressive canine's attack on the competition and demonstrate that the perceived competition will not be allowed to affect you. On the other hand, no matter how hard I work I will not be able to force a dog that is not affectionate to adore someone. With thirty-three years of experience as a professional dog trainer, I still wouldn't be able to teach a family pet that is averse to physical contact to long for it. Managing a territorial dog's hostility means removing the reward from a conduct he is naturally inclined to follow, while at the same time reducing his opportunities for this inherent stimulation. Managing intolerance aggression means teaching a dog to accept what he may intrinsically detest, which is a far cry from teaching him to want what he dislikes. So on my first consultation with the owner of an intolerant dog, we talk about the differences between tolerate, like or accept and want. Realistic ambitions set the parameters for satisfied dog owners and happy canines.

Unlike many types of hostile behavior, I see intolerance expressed early in a dog's development. It's not a shock to come across an intolerant youngster at weaning age when I evaluate a litter. When I identify a pup or an adult as intolerant, that doesn't mean he has a black mark on his soul or that he won't fit into our human society. It means this is a canine personality that may require a little more personal space than the average dog in order to be comfortable. A sensitive pet can greatly benefit from buffer zones that are established by setting up eating, elimination and relaxing areas some distance from the mainstream of activity. A touchy canine companion would not be the best choice for a high energy, affectionate owner who wants to hug and wrestle. Regardless of how important that physical aspect of interacting is to an owner, it may be asking more of a dog than he has to offer. A wise owner of a low tolerance pet would be best served by pursuing alternate avenues of interaction.

For "disturb me not" pets, I think it's prudent to establish household policies that limit opportunities for disturbance incidents. For instance, insisting on crate use for sleeping at night or setting up a comfortable dog bed on the floor for relaxing rather than allowing access to the couch. Even at a young age it's apparent some dogs, like some people, can be less tolerant when they're sleepy or uncomfortable due to pain or unfamiliar surroundings. Whether young or old a dog's tolerance level is dictated by mood or mindset; that's why sometimes closeness, bumping or petting is ok and sometimes it's not. As frustrating as it is, there's little a person can do to coerce their canine companion into enjoying something that resonates internally as repulsive. Giving an intolerant dog space, allowing him privacy while securing him peace are the first steps in managing this kind of assertive personality.

I lived with a couple of intolerant dogs in my lifetime and the most intriguing by far was my German shepherd, "Mister". He was a large fellow with a working weight (able to scale a six foot climbing wall with a three pound dumbbell in his mouth) of about ninety-five pounds with the largest head on a shepherd that I had ever seen. Mister studied everything with a confident gaze, and from the moment I met him he reminded me of a lion. He was imported to the United States from Germany when he was two years old. By the time he left Europe, he had already achieved two working titles and had been washed out of two police departments due to his handler aggression. He was a busy fellow who didn't know how to play around. Truthfully, it was his intolerant and defiant nature that landed him at my house. He was a beautiful specimen with an impressive pedigree. He never would have been turned loose from the police departments or put up for sale were it not for his hard to manage characteristics. I gladly took him on, baggage and all.

Mister didn't come with instructions, but given the very limited background that was shared with me I surmised he would be challenging to handle, at least in the beginning. It took less than fifteen minutes on the morning I picked him up to identify some of his baggage. As I mentioned at the beginning of this section, hostile protest and aggressive intolerance are often bedfellows. Mister packed a healthy portion of both. Because of his extensive police dog training, my new, intolerant and defiant companion was a considerable risk to handle. Mister had been well instructed in the art of subduing people, which meant he was skilled in using his bite and body to bring an opponent down. He was my only dog when I brought him home and I intended for him to be with me all the time at home or at the training center. Therefore, given the high risk of human injury associated with my newest charge, the top priority was raising Mister's tolerance levels so that social stability rather than volatility would be the norm. My attention was guided down a critical training path by two considerations. First, I had to compel Mister to control his hostile, visceral reactions to specific (benign) human and animal behaviors (he considered offensive) that he would be exposed to daily. Second, I needed to set up environmental controls and behavioral options for Mister that facilitated the first consideration. This is the same path I suggest for all handlers to traverse when shaping the behavior of an intolerant dog. There were two complicating factors associated with Mister's training however, that (thank goodness) most readers will not have to manage. He was a highly skilled, man stopping police dog and his normal day with me at the training center meant being surrounded by intense activity. Those two complications inspired a slow, methodical training regimen. A careful, well thought out instruction plan is always desired of course, but in Mister's case it was the difference between lifelong success and painful failure.

Muzzles are as indispensable in the intolerance aggression cases, just as they are in the hostile protest arena. Fortunately for me, most police dogs are conditioned to wear a muzzle as part of their basic training requirements. So I didn't have to delay Mister's training or work around specific issues due to muzzle unfamiliarity. **If you're the proud owner of an up and coming intolerant canine, do yourself a favor and begin muzzle conditioning yesterday!** If the companion you have at home is already experienced at throwing his aggressive weight around (like Rouge the coon hound) and is not accepting of a muzzle (like Mister), then immediately begin following the careful instruction I outlined in Rouge's training for equipment conditioning and manipulation tolerance (grooming control).

When I picked Mister up at the airport, they didn't have to tell me where he was, I could hear him a hanger away! Walking towards the thunderous barking and growling, the workers at air cargo could not have been happier to see me. Formalities were out the window, and they barely checked to verify who I was. All they cared about was expediting the removal of a frightening irritation that had been plaguing them for the ninety minutes it took me to travel to the airport. I'll never forget the supervisor in charge's comment. He said he'd always wondered what the devil looked like and now he knows, a cross between a bear and a German shepherd. Preparing for Mister's inevitable escape, they had stacked boxes all around his crate in an attempt to barricade him in. I couldn't help but laugh at their improvised five foot wall, thinking he would have easily jumped that without so much as disturbing a box. At least the barrier served as their psychological relief until I arrived.

I didn't get to liberate Mister from his crate at the airport because they begged me to load him up and risk life and limb elsewhere. So it wasn't until we were safely home at the training center that I could properly orchestrate his release. Although Mister was very eager to get out of his crate to stretch his legs and eliminate (that worked for me), he neither knew nor trusted me (that worked against me). In order to safely take a hold of Mister as he exited his confinement, I employed the leash in a noose technique that I described earlier in this section. Although muzzle trained, he wasn't wearing one during his flight and I sure wasn't in a position to put one on him at that moment. Readying my leash, I slowly opened the gate to his crate. I held the gate firmly in place with my legs so Mister had just enough opening to squeeze his bear size noggin through. By slowing down his exit, I increased the odds of getting the leash loop over his nose. Although grumbling, I could see Mister's gaze was straight ahead (in anticipation of long awaited freedom) rather than fixed on my face preparing for confrontation. This was a small but significant indication that our relationship had a chance to begin without confrontation. Preparing for the worst, I recruited help to carry Mister (crated) to a large inside dog pen, inside of which we were now closed. This way if the bear size dog did overpower me by charging from his crate or if I failed to loop him properly, at least the potentially volatile situation was contained in a secure, small area. Thinking ahead, and being somewhat seasoned by similar situations, I had placed a pan of food, a pan of water and a ball on the floor a short distance in front of the crate. This is a simple brain over brawn approach to acquiring a handling edge.

    The loop slipped smoothly over Mister's head as he made a bee line for the water pan and the food. He grabbed the ball as he swallowed the last bite of food. All of the incentives worked better than I had planned, especially since the introduction ended with a mouth full of ball (which kept him quite satisfied while we made our way outside to eliminate). Working with Mister on his disturbance aggression meant sooner rather than later, he and I were going to encounter a rough road that probably would come up quickly. I do practice what I preach by setting up a pleasant drinking, feeding and walking start (a positive first impression) which would be a tremendous benefit in aiding Mister's recovery from deterrents associated with inappropriate hostility (that were surely on the way). On our walk I was able to slide the all important slip collar over his head when we stopped for a long bladder evacuation (another instance of grabbing a little handling advantage). Mister and I really were off to a good start now: good drinks, good eats, good elimination, good walk, a little good ball play and good equipment in place. I was more than pleased with the first training session and yes these initial moments he and I spent together in fundamental activities were actual relationship building, which is the essence of dog training. Remember, regardless of how rudimentary you intend the first training session for your dog to be, set the foundation for success by careful planning, preparing and executing.

    After one day of handling Mister, all my concerns of possible, psychological deficiencies melted away. I assessed him as: clear minded, serious, confident, assertive and happy. So twenty-four hours of interaction led me to one simple truth; Mister was born with a canine personality that didn't tolerate much nonsense and he could back up his sentiment (for some reason this combination of canine characteristics has always appealed to me). Somewhere around day number three, my fast adapting new companion felt comfortable enough to challenge me on one of his intolerance rules. Until that point, I had handled Mister carefully (slow steady movements with only minimal physical contact) and lightly (short sessions with few demands) even while playing with a ball. At this point in our relationship, however, because of familiarity and fondness, I felt free to speed up our activities and include more natural physical interaction. I remember vividly engaging Mister in a series of ball retrieve exercises which understandably stimulated him. After a final toss and retrieve I was concluding the play session with vigorous physical petting for a cooperative effort, when Mister demonstrated that he'd reached his fill of my affection. Apparently primed for more action, he wasn't quite ready for the activity to be over. Keep in mind, up to the moment my hand stroked Mister one too many times, life was good for both of us. Tail wagging, playful barking and laughing best illustrate the scene leading up to the disturbance.

Regardless of the good time we'd been having, when my hand touched Mister's withers one more time than he enjoyed, his tail stiffened, his playful bark was replaced by a deep guttural growl. At that moment he looked straight into my eyes with confidence and authority. Mister didn't give me time to finish the final pat before he lunged to deliver his disapproving bite. This was a memorable experience in my career where I was so glad to be a "by the book" (even if it's my book) trainer. I was handling Mister with a sturdy leather leash (which this early in our relationship never left my hand) attached to a professional grade, steel slip collar. Instinctively, I kept one hundred percent of my attention directed toward the formidable student. Following the rule of utilizing quality equipment, nothing came apart when I needed it most. Following the rule of attentiveness, especially when handling aggressive dogs, I bought myself a little time. In the flash of Mister's attack I was pulling my left hand off his shoulder and raising the leash with my right hand for an extended correction as fast as my fast twitch muscles would twitch. At the time, it felt like my arms were moving in mud. I couldn't get my left hand on the leash fast enough to prevent Mister from grabbing a mouthful of shirt, but my right arm did a wonderful job of keeping that small brown bear off my body, and that's all that really mattered. Now with two arms devoted to the extended correction, I was able to effectively get Mister to release what was left of my shirt and somewhat settle. Before I released my two hand grip and fully slackened the leash after a fifteen count extension, I tested Mister's state of mind by pushing into his body with my legs enough to alter a change in his position. This way he would either display a compliant attitude and quietly adjust, or he would reveal a lingering intolerant mindset with vocal complaints. A test like this helps a handler decide when it's safe to lower his guard. I didn't really have a chance to even lean against Mister before he came at me again with a confrontational bite attempt. **A couple moments of settling was all he needed to regain his breath and confidence for another charge. That's why it's prudent to test an assertive, canine personality like Mister's before assuming that the lesson is learned and all is well.**

After another ten count extended correction, I again tested with a steady push. This time my winded companion was inclined to scoot over without complaining which opened the door for me to carefully return to the petting he had so rudely interrupted with hostility. **I can't stress enough how important it is in successfully managing aggression to immediately return to the task (once hostility has been quelled) the dog set out to disrupt with his hostile behavior.** All I needed or wanted to prove by returning to the petting was that his aggression didn't work to control handlers any longer. I needed to convince this bear of a dog that hostile assertive action associated with the friendly caress of his new team leader was not going to be allowed. However, aggressive action associated with a violent intruder breaking into the house, would be allowed by the team captain.

Although I needed to reinforce the new policies, I didn't want to torture Mister with affection he didn't appreciate. So once he demonstrated a positive change in plan (application of self control while I stroked him) I instantly stopped petting him and ended the exercise session with a pleasant walk and drink (interaction associated with the positive, seminal moments in our relationship building process). This return to familiar pleasantness before putting Mister away dramatically aided in his recovery from the negative experience centered on his failed attempt to establish policy. So when you set out to work with an assertive dog like Mister, exert the effort to begin and end every training session with pleasant interaction. What you gain from this effort is a noticeably happier and more cooperative student as training progresses. There is method in my madness!

Given that Mister finds some normal human-dog contact disturbing, his initial training was all about compelling him to practice restraint when faced with these benign encounters. With intolerant canine personalities, it's the primary handler's responsibility to identify possible trouble spots in daily life and act accordingly. **The primary handler must control the environment (preventing outsiders from over stepping their bounds, adjust the dog's modus operandi, putting the canine student in a secure place, etc.). The handler-in-charge should supervise the dog-in-training (utilizing proper handling gear, maintaining a manageable proximity to the dog, supplying both positive and negative consequences in a timely and meaningful manner, etc.) at all times.** Think of three steps when you set out to manage any kind of aggressive canine behavior: 1) identify, 2) control and 3) supervise.

It actually took several weeks for Mister to get comfortable with (not crave) my style of petting upon the completion of an exercise, but he eventually did come to expect and somewhat enjoy it. Although affectionate in his own way (insisted on being close to me, wild barking and jumping when I would return from being away, whining and pacing when I had to leave him), he never really craved my touch like my current companion Hector does. That had to be ok with me because that's how Mister was born to be. If I expected him to be something else, that would be a flaw in my desire and not a flaw in his potential. Remember this line of thinking when you are relating to an intolerant canine personality at home. Everyone will be happier and more content if you do.

Mister had one other sticky, intolerant behavior I had to address, and that was pushiness at doorways. He had never really been a house dog before, so good manners at doorways were not much of an issue back in Germany. No policies had ever been set on how he should give way and defer to handlers (not that he would have bought into it anyway). Like most dogs, he wanted to be the first out the door in order to survey the landscape for possible excitement. He also greatly enjoyed his role as a guardian and jumped at any chance to act as such. Unfortunately, I was not afforded the luxury to wrap up Mister's petting intolerance before having to tackle this negative and assertive behavior at doorways. For a number of days early in our relationship, Mister and I had regular confrontations on a couple of fronts. To say the least, he kept me on my toes. In Mister's world, squeezing past him to get through a doorway first wasn't going to happen. Trying to move him back or to the side and let someone in or out wasn't happening either. He's what one might call a canine control freak! My next task was to specifically address Mister's hostility surrounding doorways and the normal traffic found there.

An obvious starting point in quashing Mister's aggression at doorways was first teaching him to automatically wait at an exposed threshold when a door or gate opened. Again, I'm going to refer back to the basic handling manners I wrote about in my obedience book. Exercise number four in that book is Door Control. This is a must in self restraint for any family dog, especially if there is any kind of hostile behavior to deal with. Given Mister's newness to my house and family, his sleeping and resting place was a secure crate in my laundry room. That meant door control training for him began with his crate gate before I had an opportunity to put a leash on him.

Excited to get up and out like most dogs are in the morning, Mister was inclined to charge through the barely unlatched gate way before I was ready for him to come out. The first few mornings I let him squeeze his head through the partially opened gate so I could loop him with my leash. By about the fourth morning I adjusted that strategy by slowly opening the gate and then quickly closing it, intentionally bumping his nose in the process. Since the leash was not yet attached to his collar, my plan was to physically force him back into the crate without putting my hands on his body. Had I used my hands or legs to block his charge, I would have inadvertently given him that aggressive advantage I was trying to suppress.

I was fully prepared for a hostile explosion the first time I shut the gate on his nose. After I forcefully closed the gate, I held it securely with my feet and hands so regardless of his hot tempered determination he would not be able to force his way out. To my surprise, Mister's initial reaction was actually one of shock and disbelief, not fury. With a priceless facial expression and the gate still pushed against his nose, Mister directed his calm, confident stare right into my eyes. He didn't need the power of speech to say "You didn't just slam that gate in my face, did you?" He wasn't so shocked the second time the experience came around. As I slowly opened the gate, Mister was contemplating not lunging so I attempted to reward him with a soothing, "Good boy!" I didn't quite get "good" out of my mouth before he charged the gate with full force. Again, I shut the gate on his nose. This time Mister was mad, and his deep guttural growl vibrated the crate (maybe the entire room) while he stared at me mulling over his counter actions. My next move was like the first two. I slowly opened the gate, and this time managed to open it nearly halfway and say, "Good boy" before the little brown bear attempted to crash the gateway. He almost got out the third time, and he had to be squeezed back into the crate. With each attempt, I opened the gate a little farther and added some food reward along the way.

Gradually the growling dissipated and his self control grew. I don't remember exactly how many repetitions it took to get Mister to patiently hold while the gate was open, but I would guess around eight or ten. Since this was the beginning of door control training, all I expected was enough waiting after the gait was opened to allow me to secure a leash and give a come on through signal like "walk", "outside" or "with me". This exercise essentially takes control of the threshold away from the dog. By directing a canine student's attention toward the handler's wishes, we consequently reduce the importance of what or who is on the other side of the doorway. This is precisely what I needed to do in order to build lasting aggression control in Mister. Successfully controlling Mister's intolerant hostility at doorways boiled down to two concepts: conveying to him I controlled doorways, and making it clear that there's nothing more important in the world than his policy setting, consequence supplying team leader.

Having introduced the policy of door control at the crate, I intended to capitalize on that momentum at the front door of the house. Keeping the momentum rolling was critical because it now was rolling in my favor, and that could translate into much less battle at the front door than I encountered at the crate. The rules associated with the front door would be identical to those connected to opening the crate. A huge advantage for me at the front door was use of the leash and collar, not to mention being able to work with Mister on his side of the doorway. Easy operation of the door, effective deterrents, and loose leash (nearly escape proof) decision time all contributed to a smooth learning experience for Mister. Just a few, aggression free attempts to rush through the door are all I had to address. So what I ended up with at the first front door session was Mister waiting (on a loose leash) for permission to cross the threshold while the door stood wide open. There was no going back from here. I reinforced good manners at every doorway we passed through from that moment forward. In a case of intolerance at doorways, part of the solution lies in exchanging one set of habits for another. Replace the habit of assertively pushing forward to control a doorway with the habit of passively waiting for permission to move forward, relinquishing control of the doorway.

Gaining physical control of the doorway was a relatively simple process. The next two parts were a little more challenging. Crowding the doorway is how you should think of the second step in the door control progression. Now that Mister patiently waited for permission to cross a threshold, I had to get him accustomed to other people and dogs passing by us at the doorway while he and I waited quietly. No commands were needed here. I simply reinforced loose leash composure within the proximity of the threshold, and for Mister that meant not allowing him to pass through the doorway or bother anyone as they passed. It was very difficult for a confident, assertive personality like Mister to passively standby while others explored all the things he wanted to investigate first. That is the very challenge that brought on his intolerance aggression in the first place. Deterring others from interfering with his plans was the sole purpose of growling and snapping. Any intolerant dog you might have at home possesses a similar agenda. Whether it be a napping peacefully on the couch plan (so don't move me) or I'm purposefully walking somewhere plan (so don't pick me up), aggression can be an effective deterrent that keeps others from interfering with the dog's plan. As always, to diminish the display of hostility, all profitable results (as the dog defines profit) from that behavior must be removed or the hostile behavior will remain.

Tolerance in the middle of congestion

In Mister's case, brining innocent outsiders (both people and dogs) into the physical contact range of a known biter meant the canine student wore a muzzle. The muzzle was no downer for Mister because he had been a working police dog, and he was well conditioned to that piece of equipment. If your intolerant dog is not conditioned to a muzzle, please do so before using it in a training scenario. Remember, muzzles allow for safe training and there is no good substitute. My helpers, both with and without dogs, were instructed to ignore Mister as they squeezed, pushed, bumped and hurried through the doorway. After single helpers made their way to and fro, we added multiple helpers with some trying to enter as others exiting at the same time. Then I set up excited visitors knocking on the door, with Mister and I greeting them while others crowded around us. Although the leash was in my hand during all these training scenarios, I did not use it as a restraining device or a steering tool. I only used the leash to administer speedy corrections as a deterrent for breaking any of the rules that were in place (the composure rule, the door control rule and the zero aggression rule). Throughout the entire training exercise, I carefully observed Mister. I was mindful not to get caught up in the business of the pedestrian traffic itself. I was ever watchful for the opportunities to reward my tough student for letting things happen, maintaining a loose leash, holding on his side of the threshold, and for turning away from a bump or a push rather than react hostilely.

For the sake of training, I positioned myself with Mister in the middle of the doorway on one side of the threshold. In other words, we represented an obstacle in the way of all the passersby that had to be dealt with. Mister accepted the single helpers coming and going without effort. Two helpers at the same time were more than he could handle. He did so well with one helper that we were all caught off guard the first time a tandem tried to pass by. Mister instantly lashed out and jammed his muzzle deep into one of the helper's thighs as they brushed against one another. The helper's name was Jim, and he coolly kept on track to demonstrate the aggressive behavior didn't work at doorways anymore either. I delivered two strong jolts with the leash and slip collar to further remove any hint of satisfaction from an inappropriate hostile display. As Jim came through for a second pass, he asked "Did I ever tell you how much I like muzzles?" Clearly without the muzzle we couldn't have been as bold with the natural physical contact. Mister just proved that he was substantially faster than we were. After the negative contact experience, my canine student wanted to completely step aside and give the passersby the full doorway. Unfortunately, stepping aside wouldn't have aided in tolerance building (consenting to congestion at doorways); it was only a move to avoid what he didn't like. So I had to pull Mister back into the action spot (center doorway), where he'd be compelled by consequences to develop the necessary self restraint. When working with an intolerant family dog, we are not trying to convince him to like the household circumstances that he finds naturally irritating. We're only compelling him to peacefully accept the normal living conditions of his particular family.

Allowing people with dogs to pass and bump without complaint

Mister asserted himself one more time during the traffic in the doorway exercise. On this specific pass, I had increased the number of helpers to three plus two dogs. Mister and I were on the inside of the doorway while one handler and dog worked their way in, and two helpers and one canine lightened Mister's spirits with pleasant chatter and a few tricks with his ball while we stood center doorway awaiting the colossal challenge in handler deference and self restraint. As the crowd approached, my bear of a student understandably tensed up. He handled himself very well as the first handler and dog brushed by us, followed closely by a lunch carrying pedestrian. As the second canine handler closed in, Mister had all he could stand and he couldn't stand any more. The handler lightly bumped into me and that was all the reason Mister needed to punish the dog that happened to be in the way. I was better prepared for this attack, but quarters were very close and my student's reflexes were shockingly fast, so thank goodness for muzzles once again. **It's worth repeating, if Mister wasn't wearing a quality, well fitted muzzle, I would not have been able to set up such realistic, close quarter training conditions.**

I instantly connected a couple of strong leash corrections to Mister's venting on the innocent canine. A point worth note here, the intensity of the handler's deterrent should match or exceed the intensity of the hostile canine's action in order to have any extinguishing effect. In addition, during the heat of the training exercise, an aggressive canine student should be offered genuine, positive feedback for any appropriate behavioral effort as soon as it's recognized. Work diligently to keep the training relationship between handler and dog balanced. The leash checks I gave Mister were strong but effective. For the balance of that instruction exercise, the remaining encounters with people and their dogs elicited no more hostility from my new companion. I did call an immediate halt to training when Mister soundly demonstrated tolerance of the natural close encounters that only minutes ago he wasn't putting up with. There were never plans of getting him to enjoy doorway control or physical contact. The objective was acceptance. As soon as Mister showed me that's where he was headed, instruction for that session was over. As is customary for me and my dogs in training, I ended Mister's learning experience at the door with play and food. I wanted him to literally walk away from that scene with a pleasant taste in his mouth.

I wasn't able to set up this kind of extensive training scenario every day, but I tried to work with someone in the doorway on a regular basis. I was fortunate to have a busy training center to take Mister to everyday, because there we never have a shortage of human and animal distractions. At my home, like yours probably, a great deal more orchestration would be required to arrange challenging training scenarios. I don't want anyone to be confused about the difference between distraction chaos and an organized, purposeful training experience. With the former, a canine student seldom garners anything but frustration. With the latter, he eventually frees himself from the need of rigorous training. Simply having a busy lifestyle with Mister meant abundant physical contact from me, and countless close encounters with others at doorways. I tried to shape as many of these everyday experiences into appreciable lessons as I could, in order to solidify his new habits of self restraint and tolerance. This momentum building strategy of incorporating daily activities into the overall training experience eventually liberated Mister from leashes and muzzles. Relentless distraction proofing, by and by, gave me the confidence to take my new companion anywhere dogs were allowed.

I admired Mister like few other dogs I've met in this lifetime. We were inseparable from the day I picked him up at the airport. No differently than your dog at home, he was far from perfect and we had issues to work on, but in the long run his strengths far outweighed his weaknesses. I thoroughly enjoyed his company every day we spent together until his departure at age eleven, when he succumbed to a series of strokes. He left my care with a clean record. No innocent beings were ever hurt by him on my watch.

Chapter Nine

Possessive Aggression

Most people have come across an avaricious or oppressive type dog at some point in their lives. I have connected the unscientific description of these two facets of aggression because the majority of possessive (greedy) canines tend to be bullies. I have, for training purposes, identified these two expressions of hostility as separate facets though, because not all socially aggressive dogs (tyrants) care about guarding treasure. So much like the relationship between defensive and territorial hostility or aggressive protest and intolerance, possessiveness and social aggression are frequently overlapping behaviors. The management of resource guarding can be a reasonably straightforward process, because the triggers for a possessive dog's hostile reactions can be clearly identified by another's approach to an item deemed valuable by the aggressor. Extinguishing the fury of a socially aggressive tyrant can be a much trickier business. Unlike the usually observable triggers of possessiveness, the triggers for bullying often lie within the mental stratagem of the oppressor, which go unseen by the outside world.

I like the concept of social aggression to describe a tyrannical personality type, as opposed to the more common notion of domination. In my opinion, the word social helps direct a trainer or primary handler to the specific issue of family member interaction. In other words, the bully's primary concern is with the rank and order of his pack, and that's what most of the internal triggers for his hostile behavior hinge on. This specific area of social hostility is where the term alpha dog (and the particulars associated with that rank) really applies in regards to behavior shaping and aggression management. To briefly summarize, the mechanics of possessive behavior are simplistic and center on the single purpose of controlling the available resources. The mechanics of social control, however, are complex and center on the multifarious aims of manipulating relationships within the pack.

A young hunting dog demonstrating possessiveness.

I'll begin this section with my strategy to manage the simplistic behavior of possessiveness, then transition into the more complex conduct of social aggression. When we talk about canine possessiveness, we're talking about a much broader spectrum of resources than food, although food products are probably the most common treasures coveted. I believe "treasure" is the best label to represent what avaricious canines are guarding because the word treasure is synonymous with value. As we all know, what one man views as trash another man may see as treasure. This is an all important observation if you're faced with the challenge of extinguishing canine hostility in association with possessiveness. Hoarding, guarding, and coveting all have to do with value. In the past three decades, I don't think there's been a single week at the training center without a possessive dog to deal with. We've helped dog owners take control of every conceivable representation of a prize, ranging from dead birds and mice to feed and water pans, raw hide bones, bottle caps, kid's toys, dirty underwear, human food, leashes and collars, outside trash, half chewed sticks, garbage out of the can, dog toys, dog bedding, shoes, infant accessories (especially dirty diapers), litter box findings, and of course dog food and treats. These are all items I've actually had to work with in order to address a greedy dog's aggression, true bones of contention one might say! Most of those cataloged items wouldn't be considered food or a true resource in regards to survival or reproduction. However, I regularly come across dogs more than willing to fight over any given article on that long list. Perceived (not necessarily real) value determines whether or not an object is worth fighting for. That's why people are often caught off balance by a possessive dog's hostile position over an insignificant article. The real concern is not how or why a dog assigns worth to a particular article, but the fact he feels justified and is willing to challenge his team leader under the right conditions.

A hunting dog learning to give.

There's one little rascal that comes to mind when I think of tough treasure guarding, "Ninja". I met him when he was just a youngster, barely nine weeks old. Ninja was pure Border collie out of working stock. Both the sire and dam were accomplished herding dogs, and they combined their genetic material to produce a litter of "go getters" that weren't afraid of confrontation. Ninja belonged to my lead trainer, Dave, who took him on as a family pet and herding dog. Dave didn't have Ninja long before the young Border collie demonstrated that he wasn't afraid to take care of business. The business Ninja was taking care of was a raw chicken thigh, and he was intense about his initial introduction to raw feeding.

Dave called me the first evening he offered his new companion the all natural food and said, "I think I brought home a genuine black and white challenge." Most dogs coming from kibble feeding, whether young or old, usually need some exposure to raw meat before they feel comfortable tearing in. Ninja didn't! As Dave lowered the feeding pan containing the thigh, his new companion jumped for joy and knocked over the pan sending the chicken thigh to the floor. Naturally, Dave went after the greasy chicken part to return it to the pan, but he didn't move faster than Ninja who snatched up the raw meat and commenced to partake. Dave still wanted the greasy meat back in the pan, but when he attempted to wrest it free from his cute and "innocent" puppy, Ninja made a ferocious stand. Dave's not yet twelve inch high, fifteen pound companion was growling with the chicken thigh locked in his jaws. Boldly looking into his team captain's eyes, Ninja was daring Dave to press on with his plan to retrieve the thigh.

There was no leash on Ninja's collar during this feeding because Dave had never witnessed a hint of possessive hostility from his pup over anything before, including his regular kibble dinner and hand fed jerky treats. It was obvious from Ninja's instant willingness to fight over the chicken that the potential for possessiveness had always been there. Ninja simply hadn't come across anything worth fighting for until he was offered raw meat. With a little maneuvering, Dave was able to take hold of his pup's collar. He said trying to pull Ninja from the chicken thigh was like trying to pull a piranha from a feeding frenzy. Dave did eventually regain the thigh and put it away for another day (smart move on his part), because he wanted to consult with me before offering Ninja his next raw meal.

The next raw meal came a few days after the now notorious "chicken thigh standoff". We purposefully set this feeding up at the training center so that I could offer assistance if needed. I gave Dave plenty of room to operate because I didn't want Ninja to feel too pressured and become bashful about his hostile display. I wanted to see the young Border collie at his ferocious best. As Dave was getting things ready in our rear training room, it was difficult not to laugh at the situation given the young age and small stature of his black and white spitfire. That was until Ninja got a whiff of another piece of chicken. Then I actually laughed at myself for thinking this tough little herding dog might in some way become too timid or self-conscious to fight over a legitimate treasure. Ninja showed right away that he didn't care who stood between him and the chicken. As Dave was cutting the chicken into small pieces, Ninja was jumping, spinning and barking at anyone who'd listen, determined to have another shot at some raw meat.

Ninja is not about to relinquish the chicken quarter without an extended correction

Dave and I feel the same way about being knocked off balance by an aggressive dog (even if it's your own young pup); it really doesn't matter why the assertive behavior was directed our way, "bite me once shame on you, bite me twice shame on me!" So for Ninja's second exposure to raw meat, Dave was better prepared. He and I put together a strategy the night before which included a leash and collar for his Border collie. Cutting the chicken into multiple small pieces was also part of the training plan. I wanted Dave to have repeated opportunities to work on proper etiquette, hence a number of bite size pieces of chicken to practice with each feeding until the possessiveness was under control. Proper etiquette in this case was going to center on waiting with a loose leash for permission to eat, and ceasing to eat on command. Our intention was to set Ninja up for success by introducing the new policy with his traditional kibble. The kibble was only somewhat interesting and didn't hold the value of raw meat, which he was hysterical about. So accepting the new rules of waiting, starting and stopping according to Dave's direction was much more palatable with the kibble than it was with the chicken. Having the raw chicken pieces within sight and smell of the kibble feeding station was an integral part of our overall scheme. I wanted Ninja to think about raw meat and desire raw meat while he developed and practiced dinner etiquette. By practicing this way, we were building a loose association between the chicken and self control from the very beginning of training. Our hope was to lessen the intensity of any future battles over raw meat treasures.

Before I get into the details of Ninja's first structured feeding, I need to go over the particulars of the "drop" or "give" command. **A handler, of course, can designate any word or signal he likes for this exercise as long as the meaning of the directive is clear. Release what you have, let go of what you have, give me what you have, or cease possessing what you have. Along with "forward", "wait", "come", and "take", "drop" is one of the initial five responsibilities I convey to my personal dogs. This concept of "give it up" is defining in regards to the human-animal relationship. There should be no delay in its introduction.** Like me, Dave began Ninja's "give" instruction in the first weeks of their relationship. Working with toys and tugs initially, by the time of this possessive incident, Ninja already responded consistently to giving up tantalizing, chew bones on command. So in his mind there was no real ambiguity surrounding this concept of release, and we counted on that understanding when we set out to extinguish his avaricious behavior. The drop command is a critical tool in the management of possessiveness because it substantially reduces conflict at the moment when a treasure needs to be relinquished. If the release directive has been taught and practiced to a level of habit or reflexive response, no matter how determined a greedy canine might be, he will have a difficult time resisting standard operating procedure even when faced with the release of a special treasure.

When properly taught, "drop" means give up what you have for something else positive that the team captain will deliver. In the case of releasing a ball for example, I encourage my new canine student to drop one ball to fetch another one. Another example of positive release training is giving up the tug rope for a food treat. That is the customary way I end a playful tug-o-war session with a pup or an adult. As a side note, I feel it's good for the dog's confidence and healthful for the human-animal relationship to allow the dog to win at the contest now and then. In regards to the often discussed negative side of tug-o-war and wrestling, the fostering of malicious behavior, I've found that as long as the team leader retains overall control of the situation by enforcing "drop" and "enough" directives (utilizing leash and collar action as necessary), there is seldom any unwanted conduct created by this kind of play.

Until the introduction of the raw chicken thigh, Dave had no reason to form a rigid feeding regimen for his Border collie. Only after Ninja's display of aggression did his dinner experience become regulated and evolve into a training session. There's no need to harass an animal during his feeding period to prove that you're the boss. **If there is no apparent possessive or intolerant hostility issue surrounding the feeding event, don't create one by unnaturally and unfairly disturbing your dog during this otherwise pleasant experience.** Think of it this way, unless your dog throws down the gauntlet, let him peacefully enjoy his dinner.

Ninja's first structured feeding began with a few minutes of toy and bone "drop" exercises before any food was brought out. Dave ran through the gamut of take and give tasks: catch a ball then release it on command to catch another, take one bone and drop it on command for another, and he finished with a short tug-o-war game with Ninja's favorite toy, a flexible flying disc (the very object that gets him in trouble a little later in the Border collie story). For the most part, the take and give practice went well. As planned,

Ninja was wearing a slip chain collar and a six foot long, half inch wide leather leash that he drug around during the exercises. Dave had to use the leash a couple of times to thwart his collie's attempts to impatiently grab an item he just dropped before another item was available. Part of the "drop" command's meaning to the dog should be, once the item is dropped it's no longer yours unless and until the primary handler gives it back. The drop exercise for the canine student is a blend of patience, anticipation, and satisfaction which all hinge on deference to the handler. Possessive hostility will be difficult to manage, if this aspect of the handler-dog relationship is not fully developed or in balance.

Once Dave had his pup's full attention it was time to offer raw food. One pan contained kibble, and one pan contained the chicken pieces. Both were placed on a chair seat, which put them in the theater of action, but just out of reach. The first task was to convince Ninja to leave the chair with the feeding pans alone. This task harkens back to the first and second exercise in my handling manners program. Dave did not use formal commands during this portion of the training session. This was specifically a canine self control exercise. I cannot stress enough that the five handling manners I teach as the foundation of basic obedience set in motion a necessary learning sequence. From the five manners, canine self control responsibilities evolve (energy and drive containment, deference to the handler, and mindfulness among distractions). These responsibilities create the ability for the dog to concentrate and focus, and acute attentiveness leads to execution and accomplishment. Dave knows these things and trains this way, but Ninja was so young when he first challenged his team captain that there had not yet been enough time to complete the sequence. Dave had barely begun training and establishing policies before he had to step in and demonstrate his ultimate authority. At Ninja's stage of maturation, the idea of a team leader other than his mama was a strange concept. Truthfully, the trouble over the raw meat would have been a conflict for Ninja even if he were in a natural dog pack setting. He was born tough and unafraid to challenge pack members over treasures, regardless of who they were.

Ninja was stimulated from his play session, and the fact that it was his normal feeding time added to his excitement. But undoubtedly, it was the smell of the chicken that pushed him to near hysteria. Dave had to make a tough stand with his pup to enforce composure and food control around the chair. It was no wonder that he ran into such an intense challenge (and surprise) when Ninja first came in contact with raw meat. The little Border collie required several sharp leash tugs to keep off the chair. Until Dave could freely move the feeding pans back and forth from the chair to the floor, there was no intention for us to advance the feeding process. Ninja was bouncing and barking, but as long as he left the feeding pans alone, I instructed Dave to ignore his young pup's antics. Given Ninja's powerful appetite and determination, not to mention his youth and newness to training in general, simply avoiding the feeding pans through self control demonstrated a herculean effort on Ninja's part (Dave did amply reward his pup for all the effort). I also knew the barking and bouncing would fade over time with continued exposure, so it was actually a non-issue.

It actually took a few minutes before Dave could offer Ninja his kibble to eat, which was the next step in the training process. The pup dove into the pan with gusto and immediately pulled his head out a little disappointed. Ninja was hoping that was the pan containing chicken. He did go right back to eating, though he occasionally looked up to check on the chicken pan. When Ninja was about a third of the way through his dinner, Dave delivered a "give" command just as we had planned the night before. What we expected from that directive was for Ninja to pull away from the pan enough to allow Dave to pick it up. It came as no real surprise (especially with raw meat still on his mind), that the determined Border collie refused to relinquish the resource. In fact, as soon as Ninja heard the command, he buried his face deeper in the pan and wrapped his front legs around it. By pushing deeper into the pan, the pup announced loudly that he knew exactly what his team captain was requesting, and he was taking the stance of resistance. Recognizing that a directive has been received and understood by a canine student is an important observation during training because it can bolster a handler's confidence when action needs to be taken. **Keep in mind, with a straight forward task**

like "give" (assuming the message was cleanly sent by the handler and clearly received by the canine student), there's only one reason for refusal. The refusal is due to defiance so take action with self-assurance. Your dog will really respect you for that decisiveness.

Dave delivered a leash correction as soon as he saw Ninja commit to possessing the feeding pan. What we witnessed was the same problematic behavior that came up over the raw chicken, only this time there was no hostile explosion to deal with. The same unacceptable, greedy conduct was seen on both occasions, but one had aggressive display and one did not. Although very forceful, Ninja was much easier to manage without the hostility, and David was reaping the rewards of a well thought out training plan. The Border collie's mind was clearer without the emotional hysteria, so he could cleanly process decisions and their associated consequences. Dave did have to work (a couple rounds of multiple leash tugs) to get his pup to relinquish the pan, but in the end Ninja took a half step back from his treasure bowl allowing his team captain to take possession. David picked up the pan, praised his pup, and gave him a morsel of chicken. In reality, he traded out one form of treasure for another, preserving that positive spin on the command "give". Does this process sound familiar? Dave was essentially repeating the same sequence of events his pup was very familiar with. Ninja was accustomed to giving up one ball for another, or giving up the flying disc for a treat.

This learning experience highlights the influence of structured play on dog training. There's no question, giving up the food was easier on Ninja because he associated the act of giving with valuable positive consequences. The pivotal word in that last statement was valuable. "Giving up" or "trading out" is only positive if the item traded for is of equal or greater value than what is already possessed. This is true until the response to "give" becomes effortless through repetition and habit, or until the dog sees the handler as the undisputed captain (through relationship development) whom he wants to please more than anything else. Once giving is habitual and once the team captain has reached full authority, "trading out" is not so important. At Ninja's stage of development, trading out was still a crucial part of the "give" equation. That's why the sequence in training steps needs to be well thought out in a possessive case like this one. For Ninja, exchanging one ball for another, or kibble for raw chicken, all represented a fair trade. In contrast, exchanging a ball for a rock or raw chicken for kibble was not a fair trade. David was developing a habitual response in his Border collie to relinquish treasures through countless, positive repetitions. Utilizing a leash and slip collar, he was following a step-by-step self control strategy to ensure the outcome of "give" was always as it should be. Daily practice of relinquishing objects on command for only a few weeks usually brings about the desired results, regardless of what needs to be given up.

After affording Ninja a brief moment to absorb what had occurred, Dave presented the food pan on the floor and signaled his attentive student to dive in once more. Like me, David uses the specific signal "chow" to indicate the dog should eat dinner. There is nothing wrong with using the same command for eating dinner that you use for grabbing a ball or tug. For example, with my previous two personal dogs I used the signal "take" to indicate grab the ball or tug and bite the "Bad Guy". I also used that same word to mean eat your dinner or special treat. Either way you decide to go with a dinner command doesn't matter so long as you remain consistent in communicating with your dog. Consistency in signaling results in clarity of thought.

Understandably, Ninja was a little hesitant to start eating even though he plainly heard David's go ahead signal, "chow". No doubt, there were a couple of thoughts running through Ninja's mind. "Are you sure you don't want any more?" and "How about chicken instead of kibble?" For a young canine student, I think it's appropriate to calmly repeat the signal with a bit of encouragement, and that's exactly what Dave did. With that, Ninja began to eat with gusto again. When he was half way through the remaining kibble, David once again issued the give command. Upon hearing the "g" part of the signal, Ninja closed in around the food pan and sped up the eating process just like he did before. Without delay, Dave applied multiple leash and collar corrections then repeated, "give." There wasn't much noticeable improvement in Ninja's willingness to relinquish the food with this second experience, or the third for that matter. It still took several rounds of commands and negative consequences before the collie stepped away from his bowl and allowed his team leader to take possession. Each time Dave followed up with praise and chicken as the consequence for Ninja's cooperation. After the third training sequence, only a few pieces of kibble remained. There weren't enough to sustain a sufficient eating period for instruction. So Ninja was free to lick his pan clean and not worry again over relinquishing his dinner for a couple of days (Ninja was on a once a day feeding schedule with food reward during training throughout the day). When working with possessive behavior that centers on a canine student's dinner, I usually advise turning every other dinner time into an instruction exercise. This allows for a peaceful and satisfying dinner to separate stressful training experiences. An alternating training rhythm with dinner possessiveness will significantly mitigate the anxiety associated with this necessary learning. Along with the alternating dinner time instruction sessions, I think it's a good policy to work on relinquishing toys, tugs, and bones every day.

The second training day began pretty much like the first one finished, which was no surprise to anyone. There was one difference to start off the second instruction day, though. Dave and I heard a low growl as Ninja hovered over his bowl to guard it this time. Ninja seemed quite sure he could wear down his team captain with tenacity alone, and he was prepared to make a tough stand over this dinner. Dave, on the other hand, was on his own mission. He must quash this aggression over raw meat before this assertive behavior bleeds over into other areas of family interaction. Because Dave works on cases like Ninja's every week, he knew, his pup's hostility would spread like a wild fire through a forest if he didn't snuff it out. Several training sessions on the second day turned out to be very productive. Ninja's growling subsided during the second round of relinquishing practice. By the final session of day two, he would stop eating and begrudgingly pull his head away from the pan enough to allow his primary handler (no one else could at this point) to take it after a single command. According to our training strategy, Dave wasn't going to adjust the instruction procedure until Ninja could easily give up his kibble on command. The adjustment I'm referring to is using raw meat in the relinquishing practice.

The third training day was relatively easy, and as usual on a regular instruction routine, day three picked up almost where day two ended (that's why a momentum building schedule is so beneficial). Dave was met with resistance from his Border collie only on the first "give" command, and there was no growling associated with the pan guarding. As the training session progressed, no response to Dave's directive turned into a slow response which evolved into a fast response. By the end of day three, there was no denying the sustained, positive effects instruction was having on Ninja's behavior. Even better conduct on training day four meant high spirits for David (because he was initially very worried about the intensity of his pup's hostility), and changing over to raw meat training was the next step.

The first raw meat practice began like the four prior kibble training meals. Ninja was wearing a leash and slip collar, and he was very excited over the two feeding pans Dave had prepared. One of the pans contained the customary pieces of raw meat used in trade (or as reward for relinquishing), and the other contained the main meal. On training day five, the main meal was a large beef bone (secured from a butcher shop) with quite a bit of meat still attached. This prize of meat and bone was small enough to fit in the regular feeding pan, but large enough to prevent Ninja from consuming it quickly.

During the first attempt at this exercise, Dave was in the act of placing the main meal on the floor when Ninja (overwhelmed with the excitement of an all raw dinner) tried to slip in and grab a bite before receiving permission. Dave was barely fast enough with the leash to stop the highly motivated collie. Even though waiting for permission to eat kibble was a comfortable routine by that point, the fragrance of an all natural meal overwhelmed Ninja's desire to eat. Dave had a legitimate battle on his hands trying to reinforce the wait idea. Were it not for all the preparation work with the "give" command and kibble control, the raw meal exercise would have been aborted right there. Because of the self control and handler deference Dave had already established with Ninja, he was able to get his pup to hold (after three rapid leash corrections) while the main feeding pan was placed on the floor. Just as quickly as he applied the leash corrections, Dave grabbed a couple of pieces of sliced meat from the second pan and fed them to his drooling collie. Timing was everything here, both with the corrections for lunging after the main meal and with the reward of sliced meat for waiting. Had Dave not been fast enough to prevent Ninja from snatching the meal, all would not have been lost (dogs often beat us to the punch), but you can bet the fight over retrieving the stolen meal would have been intense and hostile. Owing to some adroit handling, Dave ended up reinforcing loose leash composure with his Border collie rather than wrestling his growling pup over a mouth full of raw meat. By the quick delivery of some tasty food reward for Ninja's herculean effort to contain himself, Dave was able to satisfy his pup's appetite a little bit and help him remain patient while the main meal rested on the ground in plain sight.

If you happen to be working with a similar possessive personality at home (regardless of what the treasure might be) and your canine student is able to steal his treasure out from under you, use the leash and collar to reinforce the drop command (even if there's aggressive resistance). As soon as the dog is compelled to release the item, remove it to a safer position but well within sight. Once you have regained control of the situation, revisit some preliminary take and relinquish exercises with your student. Make sure (during this remedial training) to utilize items of less value than the recently contested treasure. This preliminary instruction should be conducted within safe proximity of the highly valued article. The purpose of training within the sight and smell of the most coveted item is to gradually build a stronger association between canine self control, handler deference, and the ultimate treasure. Be prepared for your canine student to make another run at the forbidden resource at the first opportunity. If he was successful in the recent past, no matter how attentive and responsive to commands he may appear while working on preliminary control exercises, the possessive canine mind is probably cooking up a way to obtain the handler's holdings. Canis familiaris is the supreme opportunist, his maxim could be "adapt, procure and flourish." Perhaps that's why he has followed us all over the world; where Homo sapiens goes, so goes his four-legged survivor.

In truth, a second or third attempt to steal the resource at this juncture in training would be beneficial, because the primary handler must be afforded the opportunity to strengthen his policies of canine self control and relinquishing. At this point the team captain needs a new chance to prove his authority regardless of the environmental conditions, treasure value, or canine desire. Assuming the possessive dog launches another attempt at stealing the coveted prize, it is critical that the handler successfully quash these efforts in order to prevent serious undermining of the newly sanctioned "good conduct" rules. If a dog's subsequent attempts to challenge his team leader's policies reap rewards, handler beware! With each victory, the dog gains confidence as his team captain loses it, setting the stage for a canine bully style of relationship (which I will explore in the next chapter). In Ninja's case, Dave was off to a competent start. His tough little collie made a bold effort to take control of the resource, and he was completely thwarted by his team captain.

To reinforce the concept of waiting for permission to eat, Dave adjusted the meal pan on the floor and picked up the bone just to place it back in the pan, and Ninja was required to watch patiently. It doesn't take a lot of dog training experience to predict the outcome in a situation like this. If Dave didn't carry enough authority as team leader to keep his pup from charging toward the pan without permission, he wouldn't have any chance at getting his voracious collie to drop the delicacy on command. Until Ninja could comfortably contain himself around the pan while Dave manipulated the meal, there was no plan to move forward in the feeding process. In a sound dog training program, Ninja was receiving rewards for good efforts at being patient. Not only was Dave soothing his young student with verbal praise and physical petting, he was also filling Ninja's belly with the prepared meat pieces.

There were a couple of moments during the training exercise where the Border collie gave into temptation and tried to slip around his handler's back or under a chair to snag the juicy bone. Dave was always ready and consistently redirected Ninja's focus away from the prize with multiple, rapid leash tugs. In only a few minutes I saw an excited pup maintain restraint-free control while enjoying raw meat delicacies, but now he deferred to his primary handler over the ownership of a pan full of treasure sitting by his feet. Dave and I agreed, that this brief instruction session was very successful and should close out with no opportunity to feast on the main meal. I believe it's detrimental to the overall flow of training progression to cap a significant amount of positive effort with a negative battle, even when the handler comes out on top. Given the fact that Dave's collie was exceptionally tenacious, it would have been a mistake to give him a chance to demonstrate how tough he was after so much compliant progress had been made. With this in mind, Dave fed Ninja the rest of the meat pieces to constitute a full dinner. The juicy butcher's bone was put away until the next feeding exercise.

Ninja demonstrated outstanding self control when presented with a repeat of the butcher's bone exercise. I would confidently say that Dave resumed training ahead of where they left off two days prior. The hungry Border collie was dancing on his feet, drooling and moaning a little bit, but he was keeping his distance from the meal pan that had already been placed on the floor. Within a couple of minutes into the exercise, Dave had fed Ninja several pieces of meat, moved the pan all around the feeding area, pet his hard working pup on the head a few times, and never once had to use the leash. The more movement Dave gave to the pan, the more attention Ninja gave to his handler. This was an outstanding illustration of a bright student conquering a once overwhelming challenge, by applying all the good conduct tools he acquired through diligent instruction. The daily "take and give" training exercises, regular practice with the five basic handling manners, and a palatable step by step treasure (raw meat) control strategy was paying off for Dave. Of course, the biggest test lies ahead. Dave must allow Ninja to enjoy on the butcher's bone for a bit, and then have him drop the treasure on command. That test was set up on the following training day because I wanted this session to end on a positive note.

At last, the moment of truth had arrived for Dave and Ninja. Nothing changed in the feeding protocol throughout the training process. Every dinner routine felt the same for Ninja and that was a crucial element in our training strategy. No difference in feel plus no difference in rules leads to no difference in behavior. Preparing for Ninja's greatest challenge, Dave practiced a few relinquishing exercises with a flying disc and rawhide bone immediately prior to bringing out the dinner pans. Dave set the butcher's bone pan on the floor as usual. He tested Ninja's composure, which he handled in stellar fashion. After spending several minutes moving the pan around, praising Ninja, and feeding him some meat pieces, Dave pushed the pan towards his patient pup and said "chow". The Border collie needed a little reassurance before he felt comfortable enough to dig in, which is perfectly understandable given the tremendous challenge it's been for him to turn his mind off of the irresistible fare. Once Ninja was convinced he had actually received a green light, he snatched the bone from the pan so fast that he was a black and white blur. I think that was the fastest I've ever seen a living being move, including watching a snake strike.

Ninja tried to exit the room with his prize, but Dave (pretty quick in his own right) stepped on the trailing leash (that's why it's attached) and tugged his collie back into the eating area. We both agreed before the lesson that began Ninja's first possession of the bone needed to be very brief. We didn't want Ninja to get too comfortable with the long awaited pleasure. Calmly, Dave told Ninja to "give". Upon hearing the directive, Ninja instantly stopped pulling bits of meat off the bone and shoved the whole thing in his mouth. Dave didn't wait another moment to see where the situation would go next. He did exactly what I would have done and applied a calm, steady extended correction. The tough little collie made no sound but just clinched tightly to his treasure. Ninja's eyes were glued to Dave's. A true standoff! After several seconds the Border collie released his grip, and the delicacy rolled on to the floor. As Dave returned slack to the leash and began to praise his semi-cooperative student, Ninja lunged for the bone. Before he made contact, Dave caught him with a strong leash tug and prevented Ninja's access to the treasure. After failing to grab the bone a second time, the collie settled back into loose leash composure. This allowed Dave to return to the bone to the pan and move the treasure about, testing Ninja's resolve. When Dave was convinced his student again had reached a state of comfortable, self control after appropriate praise and food reward, he slid the meal pan towards his eager student and gave him the green light to eat. Ninja didn't delay in going to work on the bone. Since this was a dinner devoted to training (not the typical free to eat dinner), and because the Border collie was still having difficulty giving up special items when told, we only allowed Ninja a short possession time before issuing the relinquish signal. **Keep in mind, when working with a possessive canine at home, that a brief ownership strategy will help in getting the dog-in-training to let go of a coveted item, and there's no such thing as a handler having too much advantage!**

This time when Dave told his little friend to turn over the treasure, Ninja stopped chewing on the bone but hovered over the top of it, completely covering the meal with his head. That was Ninja's attempt to placate Dave and still keep the bone. The handler should view the hovering behavior as the same greedy conduct as clinching the treasure with his greedy white teeth. With this in mind, Dave applied two quick leash tugs to back his pup off the feeding pan. Ninja did step back just enough to expose the pan. This was not as far as we would have liked, but this showed effort in the right direction. Dave appropriately praised and fed Ninja as a reward.

If you happen to be working with a dog at home that is serious about aggressive contact, be very careful about reaching in to pick up or move a treasure from underneath the assertive student's guarded watch. Because Ninja is an assertive canine with low bite inhibition (no compunction over grabbing with his teeth whatever he deems necessary), Dave reached into Ninja's personal space to take ownership of the pan using his shoe, leaving both his hands free to clasp the leash. Fully prepared for the worst case scenario of Ninja grabbing a mouthful of boot (much easier to work with than a mouthful of hand), Dave insisted on his Border collie maintaining loose leash composure while he scooted the treasure around.

In this wrap up stage of possessive hostility management, there are several important concepts to note. **First of all, instruction is most effective without the use of formal commands that dispense a large portion of canine good behavior responsibility on the handler.** So as tempted as Dave may have been to help secure Ninja with leash restraint, a "stay" command, or a threatening, "leave it," he was far better off in the long run to compel his pup (through the association of consequences) to develop the skill of self control. **The second concept of note is the all important learning tool of loose leash handling.** By affording Ninja enough slack leash to feel autonomous,

Dave is actually shaping the way his pup makes decisions. Through guided instruction and repetition, along with a student's freedom to experience the consequences of their decisions, a handler is capable of bringing about habitual, positive decision making in his dog. The end result reduces the need for constant handler supervision and training equipment.

Restraint free handling leads us to the third significant concept in controlling the avaricious canine. In an unequivocal manner, Dave needed to convey to Ninja (without leash restraint) "stand down," the treasure belongs to the team leader after the relinquish command is issued. So with the confidence and conviction of a team captain, Dave had to reach in and take ownership of the treasure even though he was at risk of his Border collie's retaliation. If the handler of an assertively possessive canine comes across as trepid in his manner, the confident student will no doubt view this as a weakness that could be exploited. **Timidity in handling can actually lure a hostile canine personality into action. The flip side of this coin, aggressive handling can act as a catalyst to bring out unnecessary combativeness in a dog. Calm, focused, pleasant, yet firm, handling describes the nature of an ideal trainer.**

Knowing this, Dave reached for the pan with his foot so that he could be deliberate about taking ownership of the meal pan while minimizing risk of serious injury at the same time. The instant Dave's boot made contact with the pan, Ninja grabbed leather faster than a cat grabs a mouse. The collie's bold behavior called for an instant extended correction which Dave calmly and effectively applied. After returning slack to Ninja's leash, Dave reached in with his foot once more to scoot the pan. As soon as the boot made contact with the treasure, Ninja lurched closer to the pan giving his handler the opportunity to back him off (with multiple leash tugs) to a more comfortable distance. The rapid leash corrections were impactful, and led to Ninja's yielding ground. Dave continued moving the pan around, seizing the opportunity to reinforce the change in ownership idea while providing genuine praise (including food reward) for Ninja's deference to the handler. Eventually Dave slid the pan over to his stationary foot where he could comfortably pick it up. In less than half a minute, the pan was again placed on the ground while Ninja patiently waited for his go ahead signal. When

Dave told his pup to "chow" there was no hesitation, which demonstrated the collie's newly found comfort with the give and take routine. After no more than two minutes of eating time, Dave issued the (very familiar by now) give command and this time he received the appropriate response he'd been working towards for several days. With one command and not much mental debate, Ninja dramatically jumped back from his treasure almost to say, "Step in and get a piece captain!" Although laughing at his pup's theatrics, Dave was so thoroughly pleased with the complete surrender of the meal pan that he immediately gave Ninja the ultimate reward of "chow" along with all the undisturbed time needed to finish the delicious dinner. We couldn't have hoped for a better end to a training session. I thought it was appropriate to let that pleasant taste of cooperation settle into Ninja's memory for a couple of days before continuing his good conduct instruction. The follow ups to this training session were virtually free of confrontation, but for a while, Ninja held onto his dramatic retreat from the meal pan when told to "give", indicating what a surge of will power it took to let go of such a valuable treasure.

A meaty bone reward at last!

Witnessing the influence of training momentum on an intelligent pup is like watching the effects of an excited teacher on a receptive child. As Dave competently took control of the dinner time regimen, Ninja comfortably gave way to the new order of things. I want to emphasize here that dog training is a relationship building process between the canine student and a primary handler. The only sure way for a person to establish desirable, relationship rules with a dog is to engage in hands on instruction with that particular dog, (which is precisely what I've described in the case of Dave and his Border collie). David's wife, on the other hand, did not participate in Ninja's instruction. Therefore, she had nowhere near the control over the collie that Dave had. Ninja's relationship with David's wife was founded on an isolated set of rules which did not include a clean "take" and "give" arrangement. So this meant when the tough minded Border collie came across a special treasure, he was no more likely to turn that prize over to the female head of house than he would be to a stranger. In general dogs can accept multiple team leaders, but each unique handler-canine relationship will be grounded on rules cultivated during instruction. I will say each time a set of rules is established between a canine student and a team captain, it does become markedly easier to duplicate those guidelines with subsequent primary handlers who are willing to work with the dog-in-training. At the time of this writing, David was the only team leader worthy of deference as far as his pup was concerned. So when it came to taking coveted items away from Ninja, everyone was content to wait for Dave and that should be the rule in every home where a possessive dog abides. **If you're not the true team leader for a greedy canine, DO NOT attempt to remove items from his possession.** Many well intentioned but naïve people have suffered serious injury trying to remove treasures from assertive dogs, usually because they have watched the primary handlers successfully do so. Don't forget, different relationships mean different rules which lead to different outcomes.

Ninja never returned to aggressive possessive behavior with Dave over anything, but there was a brief stint of possessiveness involving a flying disc (the favorite toy) and Ninja's house brother, a five year old, German shepherd named "Boss." Even fully grown, Ninja was no more than half of Boss's size, but that didn't matter when it came to a treasure like the flying disc. As the little collie matured, he began to boldly storm in and take the disc from his larger counterpart anytime the opportunity arose, controlling the disc as if it were his alone. Boss thought it was great fun racing Ninja for the disc, but the collie viewed the whole event as business he needed to take care of, because the disc was his after all. I think it's natural as a multiple dog owner to view some innocent competition between house pets as healthful and entertaining. But never forget, friendly competition will always be a slippery slope leading to serious or unfriendly battles. If one of the family dogs has a personality like Ninja's, then friendly competition may never be part of the daily dynamic. There are countless, normal, canine personalities that are just too serious to enjoy light contests, and that really is ok. In fact, there are countless serious human beings with similar serious personalities who don't play very well either. For everyone's benefit, personalities like these should avoid the competition arena and leave that sort of activity to the lighter of heart.

Ninja patiently waiting his turn while Boss runs down the disc

Chasing and catching the disc is David's choice for exercising his dogs. Although both dogs like the game, Ninja was obsessive over the exercise. Boss had no history of challenging his team leader over any possessions, and he was also trained properly to take and give on command. He really wasn't a problem or even a catalyst in this situation. Boss was simply a participant, or in this case, a target. Dave quickly picked up on Ninja's slide down the possessive slope before bad relations had a chance to form between the two dogs. Having laid a magnificent foundation of possessive aggression control during dinner time, Dave jumped right into his dogs' relations over the flying disc. Dave applied the rules of conduct to Ninja and Boss equally. The rules included waiting for a "take" command and immediately relinquishing with the "give" command, while in the company of direct competition (the tough part). Utilizing six foot leashes and slip collars on both dogs, it didn't take long for Dave to demonstrate that the rules of "take" and "give" carried the same meaning and responsibility in the presence of competition (another canine). There was one new consideration for the dogs when Dave was applying the directives, however. Name recognition became a very important concept when both Ninja and Boss were being worked at the same time.

Most dogs grasp the idea of their name and its importance. The actual effort in working two canines at once lies in compelling the dog whose name was not called to hold, while the house mate whose name was called is allowed to engage. So for the dogs-in-training, following the directive connected to their name is not so much an achievement of understanding as it is a feat of self control. Boss, being the senior in regards to training and the softer personality, made the exercise look easy. Ninja, on the other hand, had to honestly labor to curb his "got to have it" drive. In all fairness, the Border collie was surprisingly cooperative and focused because of the training on raw meat control. Dave was also very careful to orchestrate the training exercises to help facilitate success. For instance, Dave placed Boss on his right side and Ninja on his left so they would have some personal composure space. Dave also began the name recognition "take and give" instruction by handing the disc to the dog of choice rather than throwing it, thereby reducing the excitement and energy associated with the flying item.

Possessive Aggression

Self control always pays off with reward in the end

The sequence in training steps was straightforward. Dave issued one of his dog's names and followed it with the command "take." He then handed or barely tossed the disc for the dog of choice to grab. A moment later he'd issue the same dog's name followed by the "give" directive, all the while enforcing loose leash, self control with the dog on deck. Dave carried out this instruction with each dog's leash hand to ensure compliance. Alternating the exercises back and forth between Boss and Ninja, Dave built a legitimate control platform and smoothly transitioned into hands free (with leash or long line dragging, still attached to the slip collar) flying disc retrieve at moderate distances. The delivery and timing of both positive and negative consequences resembled the exercises in food control. If either dog crept toward the disc out of turn, Dave applied one or multiple (depending on how determined the out of turn dog was) swift, leash tugs. On the other hand, if the dog on deck exerted effort in the appropriate direction by holding (even if not perfectly done, whining or twitching was allowed) while the chosen dog fetched the disc, Dave would soothingly pet or praise the patient canine. It took several weeks, but Dave brought both his dogs into good enough focus and self control that he has ever since exercised them off leash with flying discs. Often Boss will go left while Ninja goes right chasing their designated flying treasure. Usually, each dog has their turn to fetch and then watch, but the dogs would never to go after the same disc at the same time.

Chapter Ten

Social Aggression

What constitutes a bully? As I mentioned in the previous section, a very possessive dog is often a bully in general. An assertive canine that can effectively control a treasure or successfully guard a resource is naturally led by his covetous personality, and well-developed possessive skills to extend this manipulation of family members into other social areas. Common ways (other than possessiveness) a bully expresses himself include restricting others from access to chosen spaces or expelling subordinates from stimulating interactions. Bullying usually turns into a full time job for a socially aggressive dog for a number of reasons. Foremost, there appears to be a certain amount of gratification that goes along with forcing softer personalities to stand down. If a canine tyrant has multiple family members to oppress in a variety of situations, the sheer number of strong-arm opportunities within a twenty-four hour period necessitates a continuous effort. The canine bully also seems to appreciate the reduction in effort needed to keep subordinates down if they are kept in a brow-beaten state. We have found at the training center that canine despots, like there human counter parts, are never really satisfied. Besides being profitable (in terms of resources and attention), the act of bullying is self satisfying and therefore self perpetuating. So, if you live with a pushy or controlling dog, don't expect him to settle into a state of repleteness, and don't expect his tyrannical tendencies to one day disappear. Dissolving a tyrant's authority is the only efficacious remedy to a bullying situation at home. In other words, the assertive dog's policies must be neutralized, and his ability to administer deterrents or punishments must be removed. That's what this section of the book is all about.

"Abbie" was a bully before training, now she hunts for wild boar

Socially aggressive is the term I've designated to represent the group of dogs that tend to specifically obsess over controlling family members. As I've mentioned throughout this training guide, the eight, specific facets of aggression depicted are not mutually exclusive one to the other. Categorizing a dog as socially aggressive doesn't mean that hostile behavior is restricted solely to dominating members of his pack. If your household happens to harbor an energetic or overly zealous bully, it wouldn't be a bad idea to hang a sign forewarning, "Visitors beware!" or "Outsiders tread softly!" An enthusiastic dictator will naturally be inclined to subjugate all who are in a position to share with him. What follows is a case description that recently came through the training center. This particular anecdote is especially fitting here because it involves most of the methods useful in dethroning a canine dictator.

Basher's story begins at a rescue shelter. He was an eighteen month old lab mix and he was on canine death row when Josh and Julie Decker first met him. As far as the shelter's director was concerned, Basher had been returned to the shelter because of aggressive behavior for the second and final time. Two different families made an honest effort to incorporate this teenage canine into their home, and both brought him back with the same complaint that "he was mean!" When a person first met Basher, bouncing and happy was all that you'd see. He was intelligent, interactive and hard not to like. Josh and Julie liked him enough to talk the director into giving him one more chance. Knowing they were this troubled dog's last opportunity actually served as a powerful motivator when it came to his instruction. Josh and Julie had no previous dog training experience, and they had never rehabilitated a hostile canine. None of that mattered to them because something about adopting Basher seemed right. Josh in particular was committed to reclaiming the devoted companion he thought was hiding in the lab mix.

The Deckers wasted no time in heading off hostility with their family addition. They enrolled in a generic, group style obedience class the same day they brought Basher home. It took less than three weeks for Josh to realize that Basher's hostility was a monstrous problem and a generalized obedience class was having no positive effect on his atrocious behavior. Even though at the time the Deckers couldn't identify any specific triggers for their new dog's aggression, when I first met Josh and Julie, they (in unison) introduced Basher as their canine bully. So how does this bouncy dog push the family around?

Usually I have new clients outline their troubles by first describing in factual detail the most recent hostile encounter with the dog, followed by a recount of the first aggressive behavior they witnessed, and finally a reenactment of the most severe incident. Considering Basher's short history with the Deckers, their recall of all his bad conduct was complete and full of details. Also, both Josh and Julie were in complete agreement on how hostile events unfolded, which is rare when I work with couples. Those pertinent facts can be very difficult to dredge up when a dog has lived with a family for months or years. Due to faded memories compounded by the complacency cultivated from a family's daily grind, important information about behavioral triggers and relationship dynamics seem to pass through a handler's mind unnoticed. Not so with the Deckers. They presented to me an honest assessment of Basher along with clear behavioral particulars that were on the forefront of their minds. Because of their decisive and early action, Josh and Julie were in essence helping me to assist them in setting up an effective training plan. There was one legitimate worry about the success of this case though; Josh and Julie had an active two year old daughter, Ella.

After hearing the specifics and observing Basher for nearly an hour at the initial evaluation, the crux of his hostility appeared to hinge on controlling the interaction between family members. For instance, if Josh affectionately embraced Julie or Ella, if Julie engaged Ella or Josh in playful wrestling, If either parent attempted to discipline Ella or argue among themselves, or if a toddler tantrum erupted, Basher was stimulated to rush in and shut things down. So pack member arousal or emotional intensity acted as triggers for hostility in this particular case. This kind of energy didn't disturb Basher as much as it electrified him. We see this common form of bullying come through the training center now and again. If a tyrannical personality is titillated into action, it naturally follows for that action to be some kind of controlling behavior (according to his inherent tendencies to be the boss). Often there's no more obvious target to manipulate than the source of excitement.

I've mentioned throughout the book what an important impact leadership and pack order has on canine psyche. Whether considering a wild coyote or a domestic dog, health and balance revolve around a visible leader. A natural dog or wolf family will not function well enough to propagate without an alpha to facilitate homeostasis. One can also observe in natural settings overly zealous leaders getting carried away with their intrinsic roles of preserving family equilibrium and becoming real tyrants. As far as Basher was concerned, he came into this world with a necessary set of leadership skills, and he fully intended to micro-manage his environment. But at first blush there appeared to be nothing wrong with his mental or emotional hard wiring and his ability to learn. So as instinctual as it may have felt for Basher to be the CEO of his new family, he was headed for a major, psychological adjustment in rank. With my help, the Deckers were going to build their own set of leadership skills by developing handling techniques, utilizing training gear, and establishing interaction guidelines for their canine dictator. Working as a team, we planned to smoothly usher Basher from the driver's seat to a seat all the way in the back behind Ella!

Given that Basher's primary targets for hostility were Josh and Julie, the first handling technique we discussed for their own protection as well as its unmatched function as an aggression extinguisher, was the extended correction. After a careful in depth explanation of the how and why, if I can't sell the owner of a handler aggressive dog on the use of a correction extension, I will not commit to continuing their instruction. There is unfortunately no substitute for this maneuver, if there were, I would have included it in this book. **If you happen to own a dog that just might (under the right conditions) direct some injurious hostility your way, please review Chapter Two (Handlers, Rules and Equipment), and become familiar with the details of this technique before initiating any training.** Josh and Julie were fresh out of group obedience instruction (where emotional reprimands and harsh commands were encouraged), so I went into some depth explaining why handlers should avoid expressing negative energy. Stressing that skilled handlers don't need emotional explosions to impress their canine students, and there's no room for hurt feelings when (not if) Basher challenged their authority.

With proper training, confident aggression is directed at appropriate combat

In all forms of aggression control training, reducing the intensity of the hostile dog's emotional fire is the ticket to success. Therefore the primary handler of an explosive canine must always be careful not to add fuel to this emotional blaze. This is extremely important when the initial target for an assertive dog's wrath is the primary handler whom the canine student views as subordinate. Business-like is the way the Deckers needed to handle Basher. Proving to him that it didn't matter how he appraised family member rank, if Josh and Julie conducted themselves as confident and competent leaders their dog would be compelled to follow. Scolding and barking out commands without effective reinforcement were two of the reasons Basher's hostility was growing so rapidly. At the time, the Deckers didn't know any other way to deal with their pushy canine. They were applying, to the best of their ability, what they had learned in the "generic" obedience class. Much to their credit, Josh and Julie were quick to make adjustments in their handling technique, and they had little trouble letting go of old habits while picking up new ones.

The training gear list for the Deckers was short, but every piece was essential. Basher was strong, confident, assertive and experienced. So unless and until Josh and Julie had acquired a heavy six foot leash with a dependable snap, a heavy slip collar, a quality muzzle, and a secure crate, there wasn't going to be any training at my center. No differently than embracing the idea of an extended correction and its calming effects, if investing in this indispensable gear wasn't possible or worthwhile for Josh and Julie, then Basher's training should be handed off to someone else. Working with canine bullies who don't respect authority can be risky business, and I didn't want the Deckers (or anyone else for that matter) to be hurt on my watch because of equipment malfunction. True to his promise of commitment, the day of Basher's evaluation Josh ordered a custom fit, long wear (padded and well ventilated), open mouth (to allow for panting and barking), full cheek coverage, leather muzzle with a heavy neck strap and nose band (for a secure fit). He also purchased a professional grade, extra heavy, six foot, harness leather leash with a brass snap. To go along with his professional grade leash, Josh bought a twenty-two inch long, three millimeter thick; short linked, fast acting, steel chain, slip collar that was guaranteed not to come apart. On their way home from Basher's evaluation, the Deckers stopped by a pet store and purchased an extra large, heavy gauge, plastic airline crate that would serve as their dog's secure and comfortable confinement, in place of their gated off kitchen they were currently using. Josh and Julie's actions spoke louder than any words of commitment. From the group obedience class to the early evaluation with me, through the purchase of every piece of essential gear, the Deckers demonstrated they were one hundred percent invested in Basher's training, and that's what I needed to see to be "all in" also.

Before outlining the four rules of good conduct that I felt were necessary for Basher to harmoniously integrate into his human family, I gave the Deckers some insights on muzzle conditioning that I would like to pass on to you. When first presenting the muzzle to your dog, open the neck and nose straps all the way and fold them back over the muzzle itself. Think of introducing the muzzle as a feeding trough or treat dispenser. With the straps folded back out of the way, the muzzle resembles a large, oblong cup, full of holes. Convince your canine student that it's the perfect container to eat treats from. Make a considerable deal out of readying a bit of food to place in the nose end of the muzzle. The average hungry dog watching this preparation will be more than ready to dive deeply into the odd feeding apparatus to retrieve the morsel. His opportunity should come immediately after hearing the new command, "muzzle". Set this exercise up as often as you like, since there's no worry here about practicing too much.

The process of getting your dog used to the muzzle should move along quickly. Each time I have a canine student dive in to grab his treat, I pet him with my free hand while holding the muzzle over his mouth and nose with the other hand. As I pet the dog, I also control his head and neck posture just enough to keep the muzzle in place, but not enough to create panic over restriction. With each experience, though, I hold the muzzle over the student's nose for a slightly longer period of time, using a few soothing words along the way. Smearing a little soft food inside the nose end of the muzzle for licking (while wearing) is not a bad idea either. As soon as the dog's comfort level dictates (a handful of practice sessions), pull the loosened (but still buckled) neck strap up over his ears so he can get a genuine feel for the muzzles fit. Once I'm able to pull the neck strap over the ears, I do it every time and hold the muzzle on the dog's head by the strap alone. At this stage of conditioning, I will take more liberties to adjust the nose band (on muzzles having an adjustable band running from the nose covering part of the equipment, up between the eyes and over the head, terminating with a connection into the neck strap) placement and neck strap tightness, but only for brief moments before removing the muzzle.

One of the keys to muzzle acceptance is making absolutely certain that the handler is the one that removes the apparatus, not the dog. The command "muzzle" gives a dog permission to reach in and eat the treat (in essence, put the muzzle on). A signal like "all done" can be connected to its removal. From the point in training where the neck strap is pulled over the ears, a handler needs to demonstrate, equipment removal is his responsibility, not the canine student's. Never afford your dog the opportunity to shake free of his muzzle once it's been placed on. Allowing a dog to pull free from the equipment sets a terrible precedent that will negatively affect muzzle wearing for the rest of your canine friend's days. Utilize a leash and training collar to assist in controlling the dog's head and neck posture. I have a leash and collar on my personal dogs when I teach them to catch a treat or ball. I prepare for the unexpected by habitually utilizing leashes and collars with my new students, even when teaching playful exercises like speak or jump. I would never undertake weighty instruction like stay, walking, or muzzle conditioning without a safety net!

Snugging up the neck strap and shortening the nose band (if there is one) occurs when the muzzle wearing student shows he's comfortable sitting or standing a short while (after the treat has been consumed), with your hands holding the equipment in place. It is especially important when the straps alone hold the muzzle on, that the dog not be able to lower his head and use his front feet to pull the apparatus off. Insist on loose leash composure while hanging out during this part of muzzle conditioning. In other words, don't take on the responsibility of physically holding the dog's head up to prevent unwanted removal of the muzzle. No differently than we expect and enforce our canine students to abide by a "don't chew on the chair leg rule" without physically holding him back from the chair, we'll expect and enforce (with the application of consequences as I've instructed throughout the book) acceptance of the muzzle. Next introduce the walking exercise making sure to keep the dog's head up away from his feet. Gradually but steadily, work through his entire repertoire of commands wearing his muzzle and insisting on a loose leash the entire way. Within reason, the more often your dog sports his new equipment, the more natural it will feel to him and the more comfortable he'll become.

I didn't get a chance to introduce my dog Hector to a muzzle until I took him on at three years of age. His age and assertive experience played absolutely no part in his muzzle conditioning instruction. I walked him through the process exactly as I've laid out here. With confidence I can tell you today, if I casually walk up to Hector with his muzzle attached to my equipment belt, he will insist on sticking his nose deep into the oblong container and try to put It on to enjoy a reward he believes is waiting inside. The muzzle will only represent negativity if you introduce it without a favorable approach.

Now back to the Basher story. Although there were four slightly different triggers requiring four slightly different rules of conduct in this particular case, the new policies were all about the same thing, we must help Basher improve his behavior during the occasions of family member interaction. I suggested several guidelines for Basher. The first policy was: no cutting in or joining an affectionate moment between family members unless invited. The second policy meant: no breaking up or joining wrestling matches and arguments between family members (there will be no invitations to join in this kind of interplay). The third policy stated: no assisting Josh or Julie when disciplining Ella. And the fourth policy was: no directing assertive behavior toward Ella (the obvious subordinate) of any kind for any reason. From an instructor's standpoint there was one very positive aspect to this training challenge. Three out of the four instruction scenarios we needed to set up were going to be easy to arrange. Basher's interference with disciplining Ella was going to be a tricky arrangement to set up, given the fact that Ella was too young to understand her parents acting out a discipline scenario. Convincing portrayals is what we needed to represent real life interactions. Sincere acting meant duplicating the energy or emotion of legitimate discipline and we weren't able to do that with such a young child. This meant Josh and Julie would need to be prepared for disciplining Ella and handling Basher at the same time. The Deckers did work well as a team in regards to communication and cooperation, so I didn't worry over this portion of Basher's instruction. I simply wanted to accomplish as much as we could in the other three areas as quickly as possible, in order to minimize problems when the inevitable event arose.

Official training for Basher began roughly two weeks after his initial evaluation. This starting date gave the Deckers time to receive Basher's muzzle and get him conditioned to it. Because Basher's hostility episodes were frequent and opportunities for bullying were plentiful, (not to mention the high risk of injury to Ella) the muzzle, leash, and collar were in place any time he was exposed to family interaction. We did not intend for this to be a permanent condition, but it was a necessary safety precaution during the early weeks of training. One of the safety concerns the muzzle helped alleviate was the strong possibility that a bully like Basher wasn't going to accept being corrected. More than likely, when Basher's pushy behavior is put in check, the handler taking charge must be prepared for retaliation or an aggressive protest. The muzzle will bring a sense of calm to the training scenario. So whether it be Josh or Julie who first counters Basher's interference, they will have less worry about being bitten and therefore more confidence for the instruction task at hand.

We all agreed that the first training scenario should be the easiest to orchestrate. This would give the Deckers a chance to get their feet wet (as delicately as possible) in the waters of aggression management. So the first policy (no cutting in or joining an affectionate moment between family members without invitation) was the focus of our initial instruction session. In an attempt to create a close, homey atmosphere, I decided to use my office as our training ground. **It's impossible to overstate the importance of the instruction "set up" and first impression.** Carried out correctly, one session could provide the Deckers an entirely different tone for their family dynamic than the one Basher was currently enjoying. What we needed to start things off properly was "hang out" time. Josh, Julie, Ella and Basher were all chilling out in the office. Ella had a few toys she was playing with on the floor while Josh and Julie were chatting on the sofa. On purpose, Basher was left without much to do except meander around the office. There were no chewing bones or toys for pacifiers, and no commands were allowed for assisted control. I didn't want anything to get in the way of Basher's relationship monitoring. Basher was a confident, happy fellow, so it took no time at all for him to feel perfectly relaxed in the office. That was one of the necessary ingredients for training success. I had to supervise from the waiting room by nonchalantly viewing through the doorway. The feeling of a natural family gathering was almost as important as good training equipment in this case.

At the start of the session, Josh was designated as the primary handler so he would be the one to address Basher's assertive behavior if need be. On cue, the Deckers began to feign cuddling (I think they were pretending, but it looked pretty real to me!), and like a shot Basher literally stepped all over Ella to force his way between Josh and Julie to break up their fun. Like most inexperienced handlers, Josh felt rushed to grab of the leash and pull Basher off the sofa to remedy the situation without any real corrective action as a deterrent. I told Josh this opportunity was all about supplying an effective negative consequence for an unacceptable behavior, not simply removing the dog from the location. One of the reasons we had a muzzle on Basher was to alleviate worry over possible handler injury, and allow for the necessary time and adjustments needed to impressively jolt Basher to dissuade him from repeating such an act. It's a given that Josh needed to carefully remove Basher from Ella, but once that was accomplished leash and collar tugs were a necessary follow through.

Understandably, Ella was a little upset by the occurrence, and she wanted to crawl up onto the couch to sit with her parents. We positioned Ella on the outside of Julie so that we could try and repeat the experience without having her in the middle of the melee. Basher, on the other hand, didn't appear upset at all. He didn't care much for Josh taking charge, and our canine student growled convincingly for being forced off the couch. After five minutes or so of relaxing and shaking off the previous experience, the Deckers once again began snuggling. This time they engaged with more enthusiasm to make certain they were still an attraction. It almost looked like Basher was hesitant to jump in, but that didn't last long. When he decided to go, Basher did so with more force than the first time. Josh was more prepared this time. Acting like a pro, Josh calmly but securely took hold of the leash, stood up to remove the party crasher from the sofa (who was now earnestly threatening his handler to back off), and corrected Basher a couple of times with the leash and collar. Indignant and enraged at such insolence, the canine bully jumped on Josh taking the fight right up to his face. Coaching from the sidelines, I instructed Josh to move to a calm and determined correction extension. Basher had real experience when it came to confronting people, and he wasn't the least bit intimidated by Josh's strength. Basher was fighting back for all he was worth. Close at hand, I could see Josh's determination starting to wane so I stepped in to help him with the extension. I took charge of the leash from Mr.

Decker and I continued to calm Basher with the extension as I explained to Josh and Julie that they were on the right track for rehabilitating their adoptee. With a really tough dog like Basher, I often have to step in to assist the handler and calm the situation, so this was no affront to Josh's technique. I only had to hold Basher in the extension several moments longer than what Josh had already done, but these were defining moments. Had Mr. Decker given in and returned his assertive student to a loose leash before the hostility had fully abated, Basher would have registered this as another victory in his human domination, and Josh would have had a difficult time regaining leadership status.

A great deal was riding on this initial confrontation. Basher was insisting on controlling snuggling and being the boss of the family, and Josh was insisting on being the team leader and relegating his dog to the back seat. No sooner than the hostility was extinguished and slack returned to the leash, Basher was back to relaxed tail wagging and smelling around the office. The Deckers were amazed how little the encounter upset their companion. I think most owners of aggressive dogs are shocked by their canine companion's ability to shake off confrontation in stride. For confident, assertive dogs, butting heads is not that disturbing. They see it as a natural way to work out differences no differently than Josh and Julie would view a heated discussion. Basher accepted the confrontation as a debate that he lost rather than seeing it as a cataclysmic event like most dog owners do.

With the atmosphere calm again, the Deckers were back to role playing, determined to show Basher that they would cuddle as much as they wanted and he wasn't invited. While Josh and Julie snuggled, Ella leaned against her mother hugging a stuffed animal and sucking her thumb. As the Deckers cuddled, Basher paced from one end of the little office to the other. Although he wasn't what you would describe as content, he was not bothersome. The canine despot was forging new, more acceptable behaviors. Basher was born with an abundance of energy and drive, so channeling and containing all that force required substantial effort on his part. Witnessing their new pet exercising free will to pace rather than to disrupt the family on the sofa inspired Josh (with no cue from me) to jump from the couch and lavish Basher with rewarding attention. Josh's timing and understanding of the sequential training process was far superior to my average inexperienced client. Josh left his dog to pace for long moments while the family snuggled to be sure the appropriate lesson was learned with the previous experience. Jumping from the couch too soon to reward his dog may have preempted another challenge to authority that was yet unseen in the planning stages of Basher's mind. **Waiting for noticeable, sustained commitment to acceptable conduct is a key component in aggression management. Seizing the opportunity to reward when this commitment is confirmed is just as crucial for successful hostility control.** One of my responsibilities as an instructor is to nudge clients at the right time to correct, to wait, or to praise. Mr. Decker seemed to require little prompting at these critical moments even though he was just a handling neophyte. We ran through this exercise a number of times with varying configurations of duration, intensity, location, and respites. Basher never truly relaxed, but he offered no more interference or bossing which defines for me a successful training experience.

In describing the set up of this training session, I specifically mentioned there would be no pacifiers for Basher. That restriction was only important at the initial implementation of the first policy so to channel Basher's attention toward the activity on the sofa compelled him to make a decision of "go" or "no go". Unless, and until, the student can effortlessly and consistently make the right choice, I find it best not to give them something to redirect their mental energy. In essence, using pacifiers and restraining devices or controlling commands early in aggression management training only puts off what eventually must be addressed. What must be addressed is energy containment and drive channeling. Along with those decisions, a dog must be comfortable to bring those two disciplines into reality. Once a canine student has forged a new habit of appropriate decision making in regards to "go" or "no go", offering chew items or toys as a release for displaced energy, drive, frustration, anger, or anxiety, is a beneficial training maneuver. For Basher, given his explosive hostility, hardness and determination, pacifiers were somewhere in the future when appropriate decision making came easier and after his muzzle was no longer needed.

After summarizing the day's events, I sent the Deckers home for real world application. Capitalizing on the momentum we created at the training center would be invaluable for Josh and Julie when facing their canine despot without me. Although Basher may gain confidence in his own house, he will have fresh on his mind the thwarted attempts to bully, which will reduce his determination and ferocity. **As a reader, you will not have the training center and me, so you must build your own training momentum with repeated, successive exercises with short breaks in between. Momentum should build, if it does not and you witness an increase in challenge or hostility, cease training exercises and seek out professional help immediately.** With a socially aggressive dog that targets primary handlers, the risk of personal injury can increase exponentially and must be heavily weighted in the relationship building balance.

I didn't see the Deckers and Basher until the next week when we shifted our focus to the second and third policies that entailed the higher energy scenarios of wrestling, arguing, and disciplining Ella. I wanted Josh and Julie to have a good head start in managing Basher's hostility before we tackled these more intense situations. I also wanted Basher to be well on the self control path before exposing him to this greater challenge. These scenarios were also going to be more difficult to set up with a realistic feel, so that's why we saved them until the second instruction session. This is a good strategy to employ at your home as well.

In order to draw Basher into an intense engagement between Josh and Julie, I had them leave their companion in the vehicle when they first arrived at the center for their instruction. This way we could rehearse a little and agree on a course the mock argument should take. The plan we decided on was to begin the session with the Deckers wrestling which would naturally amp up the energy and then transition into a heated discussion that would gradually rise in intensity. I had Josh and Julie located in my office again so the environment would be confined enough to force close proximity with Basher and press him into a decision making moment. In the hope that the

Deckers would be believable in their argument, I recruited Katherine (my right hand female instructor) to babysit Ella elsewhere in the training center while we carried out our task, thereby preventing the chance of her getting upset. If Josh and Julie felt a little awkward wrestling out of normal context, I couldn't tell, and neither could Basher. Almost instantly energized by the activity, he leaped into the tangle climbing up Julie's back not so much as an aggressive bully but as a wild participant. Fun loving or not, the climbing behavior was way too physical and pushy. It was certain to lead into more assertive conduct, and the Deckers had not invited him to join in.

It was Julie's turn to be the primary handler, so she did her best using the leash to back Basher off. Julie is considerably smaller than Josh and in no way as strong, so her best efforts at leash corrections only further stimulated her powerful adversary. I had Josh step in right away to help. No differently than me assisting Josh, double team if necessary, but keep the canine challenger from winning the day. It is terribly important that the assisted primary handler remain in the theater of action if at all possible. By doing that, the rescued handler picks up some respect through association with the stronger trainer, and by being part of the winning team. Basher was revved up, and consequently Josh had to deliver several stout leash and collar tugs before Basher regained self control. The good news was Basher didn't push the fight further after the sobering leash jolts, so no extended correction was needed. The moment the squabble was settled, I instructed Josh to drop the leash and regain the wrestling momentum. Basher stood on the periphery studying the two contestants, but he didn't think the wrestling was quite as stimulating or inviting as it was just a minute earlier. Everyone needed a small break after this last round of uninterrupted jostling, and this presented an opportunity to sooth Basher with rewards for his self control effort.

Stepping in and out of the high energy roles was no doubt difficult for the Deckers, but it was absolutely necessary to simulate the real interaction to enforce the new policy. Because dog training concentration and preparation can never be up to par during an actual wrestling or arguing event, it's not going to be an ideal time for Josh and Julie to shape their pet's behavior. As taxing as it may have been, acting was the only way to go.

When training continued, I felt sure the Deckers would be able to reach a heated state of discussion and possibly trigger Basher to act aggressively. So I gave Julie (who was still the designated primary handler for the day) a few suggestions on addressing hostility. I really wanted her to be able to control Basher without Josh or me having to step in. I reminded her that the muzzle was on for her protection so there should be no panic to turn the hostility off. Julie could take all the time she needed, however, early decisive action (the instant assertive behavior is recognized) and strong, impressive deterrents (rather than gradually increasing intensity) would work wonders to impress Basher. The same holds true for the bullying situation you may have at home.

With a little wrestling to warm up, the Deckers launched directly into a pretend, heated argument (their arguing was believable enough, I had to inform people in my waiting room that everything was ok and they should just move along!). From my observation point outside the office, I could see Basher's pacing had become more agitated. I tried to give Julie a "heads up" signal before there was an explosion of hostility that might catch her off guard, but she was so involved in her role that I couldn't grab her attention. I could have stepped in to instruct her but that would have disrupted the scenario so much that any learning experience for Basher would have been lost. Believable acting on Julie's part was beneficial to training. However, failing to concentrate on her primary task of monitoring the student's behavior was detrimental. Julie did not notice Basher's transition from pacing to rigid posturing (both his bristle and tail were straight up) inches from her backside. With that change in behavior, the bully had made his decision to intercede. Josh noticed the torpedo like dog zeroing in on his unsuspecting wife, and Josh tried unsuccessfully to signal her into action without stepping out of character.

Faster than a smoldering ember bursts into flames, Basher leaped at Julie in an eruption of barking and growling (the muzzle was on, so biting wasn't an option) that completely took her aback. In Julie's defense, she was admittedly intimidated by her canine adoptee so she had a lot to overcome in order to take charge of him. Julie's trepidation was all the more reason for her to take early action. Once Basher morphed into a hostile monster,

Julie would actually shut down rather than confront him. Any canine despot would take advantage of this breakdown in confidence, of course. Both Josh and I instantly stepped in to correct Basher and rescue poor Julie. She was clearly too upset by this point to effectively manage the bully, who was by then climbing all over her. In just those few short moments, Basher had really worked himself into a frenzy and hostilely came back on me for stepping in. A calm extended correction (about ten counts long) cleared his mind and settled his emotional fire.

After reassuring Julie that if she could muster even a couple moments of courage, she would be more than capable of extinguishing Basher's aggression with no help from me. I reminded her that not very long ago her husband was in this exact same position, and he pulled himself up to team leader status by mimicking my early, decisive actions and soothing reward. I also threw in a couple of extra motivators that I seem to use weekly. I put two truths on the training table for Julie. The first truth was the Decker family was undoubtedly Basher's last chance to dodge euthanasia, and if Mrs. Decker couldn't manage him without Mr. Decker, he was going back to the shelter. The second truth was if they decided to keep Basher, more often than not the only thing standing between Basher and Ella was Julie because Josh worked many hours away from home. We all agreed to one more instruction session for the day that should follow a relaxing dog walk outside. Periodically clearing the canine and human mind of negative energy is always a good idea whenever you're immersed in emotional training.

The upcoming instruction session was going to be a pivotal event for young Mrs. Decker. I had done all the instructing I could do, and Josh had done all the galvanizing that he could do. I gave Julie her marching orders: "While you're acting, peripherally study Basher's appearance for that distinct moment he commits to inappropriate conduct that always precedes his explosive behavior. Seize that initial manifestation with a ten to fifteen count extended correction, or until Basher disengages. Do not try to employ leash corrections because yours are not impressive enough and they will only serve as an irritant. Don't talk to any of us or scan the environment for onlookers while you're engaged with Basher, only focus on the one task of extinguishing his hostility. With that, Julie headed into the office with new resolve.

I genuinely felt for her because Basher was an unusually hard and tough dog. His correction threshold was through the roof, and he was more than a little stimulated by confrontation. A battle seemed to turn him on. That's why the most effective deterrent we can employ with a hostile personality like his is the calming, subduing, extended correction which removes the opportunity for stimulating confrontation and takes the fun out of fighting. Removing the fun and the victory from battle makes it (for even the most determined bully) a futile pursuit that will eventually be abandoned. With a combative personality like Basher's, it could take many months before most of the socially, aggressive behaviors fully wind down. That doesn't mean Josh and Julie aren't gaining ground by the accumulating training days. It means that a smart, successful dictator will not throw in the towel simply because he ran into some resistance.

This collie learning to strong-arm ducks with a purpose

The canine despot must come to his own conclusion after multiple, thwarted attempts to exercise rule (over a substantial period of time), the coup against his regime was successful and he no longer wields the authority that he once did. Unless your in-home bully was born a pure, alpha personality (and that's doubtful, because very few of these personalities come into the world at any given time, thank goodness), he will one day relinquish the driver's seat and comfortably settle into a passenger status. **Almost every socially aggressive dog we work with at the training center will stand down if he's met with a four prong response for a period of several months: first prong, a well thought out training plan; second prong, the utilization of appropriate equipment; third prong, effective handling techniques; and the fourth prong, the proper environmental controls.**

I've been reluctant to use the term "alpha" in this book because it's overly used. Since I did mention it, I thought I should follow with a few relevant comments. In more cases than not, this misunderstood label is inappropriate and tends to misdirect dog owners in their handling, not unlike the terms "fear aggression" (my personal favorite), "dominant" and "separation anxiety". Labeling a dog with one of these broad labels (that are hard to get away from in today's dog circles) discounts the unique and complex make up of the individuals that represent Canis familiaris. If you've picked up anything at all from this book, you should be able to appreciate the wisdom in this following statement: looking past or ignoring individualized personality traits absolutely undermines even the best training efforts.

In regards to pure, canine "alpha" personalities, they do exist. They are few and far between, however. Used as a descriptive word, "alpha" implies leader, number one, or second to none. Given, in nature there will be varying degrees of alpha qualities, which would lead to more or less effective leaders. I think it's best to think of an "alpha" dog as a canine possessing a set of well balanced characteristics, including but not limited to: courage, high intelligence, determination, aggressive assertiveness, and a high pain threshold. All of our family dogs possess some of these characteristics. Many have all the characteristics in sufficient degree to be a leader of some kind if the opportunity were thrust upon them. When I refer to a pure "alpha", I mean an individual whelped with one purpose, to be in charge. I'm talking about a canine that possesses all the necessary characteristics of leadership, in abundance. I'm talking about a dog (whether wild or domestic) that would never be satisfied with second place. He will either be in charge of his pack, destroyed trying to be in charge, or ousted, but he will never be content with any status less than "alpha".

If pure "alpha" is the characteristic make-up of your in-home bully, you can win a battle for leadership but you can't win the war. This doesn't mean there is something wrong with your dog or situation. You do not have to get rid of your "alpha" in order to live peacefully. You will, however, need to stick to the four prong response I just outlined at least until your whelped-to-be-in-charge companion reaches his peaceful geriatric years. That's not really that long is it?

I've owned a pure "alpha" once in my life and his name was "Apache". He was a pain in my rear on occasion, but a marvelous companion dog overall. I also answered his challenges with the four prong response I described to the Deckers. In fact, that's when I began to formulate such a response. Hopefully without getting too sappy, I could tell you that Apache was a very happy dog for the nine years he lived with me. He was born with a serious personality of course, but he was excited about life with me, mostly because I appreciated him the way he was. I didn't mind a challenge for leadership every several months, and neither one of us held on to negative impressions from those confrontations. We enjoyed each other's company before and after these brief battles over "alpha". So if you're lucky enough to come across such a magnificent specimen of the canine species as a pure "alpha", enjoy! You are not likely to come across another.

I'm going to pick up the Decker story with Julie walking back into the office for what's called in rodeo, the short go around (our final ride for the day in other words). Her confidence did seem to be up for this last session. Thoughts of being Basher's last chance served as a powerful motivator, because she was as determined as Josh to keep him, and that meant that she had to get over the paralyzing, intimidation hump. The Deckers jumped right into verbal battle with a little arm grabbing added in. As the two actors shuffled around the office escalating the energy, one could watch Basher from outside strategically avoid Josh while jockeying for better position to target Julie. Again, I will mention Mr. Decker had already impressed Basher with his leadership skills, so the young canine student wanted no part of a battle with him, hence the avoidance. Mrs. Decker, on the other hand, had yet to impress Basher as the team captain. She was still fair game as far as Basher was concerned; but by watching Julie sharply focus on her student while carrying on the acting, I felt a change in their relationship was coming.

Julie was now psychologically prepared for action. She was physically upright in a ready position, looking for the moment of commitment to seize. Mrs. Decker didn't have to look too long. Hard-headed Basher wasted no time attempting to finish the lesson he attempted to teach Julie during their last confrontation. Josh was only catching glimpses of Basher at this point because the student was very adept at keeping the target between them, and this meant Josh couldn't give Julie any for warning. The Deckers were moving around so much I could not grab Julie's attention either. She didn't need our help anyway. This time she noticed the pacing stop and she saw his bristle and tail go up. At the earliest possible moment, Julie turned to grab the leash. Unfortunately, Basher was already in monster mode and lunged at her at precisely the same moment, barking and growling for all he was worth. A feeling of failure instantly fell over me, thinking he got the best of her again. But with cat-like reflexes Julie had that leash extended and she was actually moving towards Basher rather than away from him. I couldn't help but cheer. It was like watching super woman fly in and snatch up a bully. Basher was hotter than a pepper for all of ten seconds but in that short time he came to grips with the fact that Mrs. Decker was now in control. With no options, he looked up at the determined and calm handler without rage in his eyes. Instead, his countenance was calm and resigned to passivity. Basher's full attention was on Julie (an up and coming team leader) and nothing else.

Basher's complete transformation from monster to respectful student is the unexaggerated beauty of an extended correction well executed. Mrs. Decker was steadfast even though her challenger thrashed about during the first moments. She kept her cool and didn't allow emotion to take over as she had done in the past. Witnessing the sustained positive effects of the extension, Julie lowered Basher's front feet back to the ground. As soon as the leash slackened, he directed a distinct, threatening grumble towards what used to be his subordinate. The moment I caught sound of that threat, I barked at Julie to give absolutely no ground here. I instructed her to quickly give the challenger a couple strong leash tugs, and if he answers that with more hostility she should apply another extended correction. With two of the crispest leash tugs Julie had ever given, Basher looked away while grumbling under his breath. With that I stepped into the office to compliment Mrs. Decker on the exquisite handling, and to prevent her from employing another extended correction for the grumbling. A correction wasn't appropriate for that head-turned grumbling conduct because that was the bully's announcement he was standing down, albeit with a little complaint on the side. This was an altogether different signal than he was sending with the threatening, eye-to-eye-contact growl. **If you happen to be working at home with a canine personality like Basher (tough, confident and assertive), keep in mind, a little negotiation is a good thing when you notice behavioral movement in the right direction. We want to send a message to the canine student that we appreciate your effort so I'm going to let that head-turned grumbling slide.**

While I was critiquing the Deckers, Basher decided to fully relax and lie down at Julie's side, presenting an excellent opportunity for her to soothe him with a few heavy stokes of her hand and some soft words. Understandably, Basher and the Deckers were showing signs of emotional fatigue, but now was the time to finish driving our point home to the waning authoritarian. After a brief step outside for a little ball play and elimination time, the Deckers set up for the last performance of the day. I desperately wanted Julie to leave the training center with a growing new dynamic between her and Basher. I was determined not to let Julie finish the training day with a lower status than her young, canine adoptee even if that meant a few more encores. I didn't tell the Deckers or Basher about my resolute course because I was afraid all three of them would have bailed out on me. Momentum was clearly in the Decker's favor now, including Julie as a primary handler. We needed to continue pushing Basher (with combative drama between Josh and Julie) to the point of decision making, until he elected (without the use of deterrent) to abstain from the volatile situation and allow his team leaders to work out their differences with no input from him. After all, it was really none of his business, and that was the point we were attempting to drive home.

No sooner than I had vacated the office, Josh takes hold of Julie by the shoulders and with loud words sits her on the couch. Basher, who was still stimulated from the ball play (one of the reasons for going outside in the first place), almost launched onto the couch after her, but managed to hold himself back. The canine student's self restraint was definitely a plus, but not enough assertive shut down to warrant praise. Although he didn't charge into the melee, he remained rigid and focused on Mrs. Decker. Without hesitation Julie jumped to her feet and took the argument back to Josh, and I felt sure this explosion of energy was the final straw on the bully's back. Julie's intensity did prove to be the impetus for action from Basher, but not what we expected. As Julie rose to her feet spewing pretend words of anger, Basher made a barking, half lunge then instantly aborted and ran out of the office. The Deckers, who were fully prepared for confrontation, were so shocked and relieved at their depot's quick departure they fell on the sofa laughing hysterically. Basher felt the change in the emotional climate instantly, and stuck his head through the office doorway to peak on his family. His tail was in a rapid submissive wag (low carriage and short swing) while he assessed the situation. What a dramatic change in behavior. Basher was sending a crystal clear signal to both Josh and Julie. "I concede. You two are the captains. Call when you need me, I dare not interrupt!" Call they did, and Basher ran over to the sofa to receive some affection and praise from both captains. Eventually we insisted on Basher remaining within proximity of the temptation while maintaining self control (like we always do), but for that exercise I couldn't have been happier with his effort.

Social Aggression

Basher finds contentment without bullying anyone

The most noteworthy accomplishment of the day was not so much that Basher quashed his own hostile behavior (albeit that was huge), but the fact that Julie brought about his change in conduct without my (or Josh's) intervention. At the training center I continuously refer to the handler/dog relationship as a dancing partnership. Someone needs to lead, and someone needs to follow. There is no way around that. Unfortunately, as the human handler, you're the designated leader. You can be taught how to lead, but no one can dance for you or else it becomes their partnership, not yours. Watching a skilled dancer glide across the floor with your dog is definitely beneficial as a demonstration. Having your dog taught to adeptly follow a dance is definitely beneficial while you're developing new skills of leadership. Ultimately, though, the handler must learn how to do his part if he harbors a true desire to dance gracefully with a canine companion.

The four weeks of instruction for Basher that followed the decisive training in my office were productive enough to allow the Deckers to permanently remove the muzzle from their companion. The exceptions to that liberty are the infrequent trips to the veterinarian where Basher wears his muzzle out of courtesy. The specific scenarios for disciplining Ella that Josh and Julie set up never really took on much life. Nearly all the aspects of aggression control were fully developed with the initial policies surrounding affectionate moments, wrestling, and adult arguments. By the time the Deckers confidently worked their way to the last policy for Basher, which forbade him from disciplining Ella, their dog was committed to self control in any situation that involved energetic or emotional interaction. If either Josh or Julie were participants in any disciplining, the presence of a team captain alone was enough to influence Basher to work on good conduct by resisting the urge to join in. But every once in a while, on days he feels especially spry, Basher will get carried away and find himself pushing into a playful, wrestling match between Josh and Julie. On occasion, when Ella is reeling from too much sugar and not enough sleep, Basher recalls a faint sense of duty, which compels him to accompany the appointed disciplinarian in need of back up. Whenever the despot's ugly face peaks out from behind Basher's otherwise, happy countenance, Josh or Julie waste no time in utilizing training gear and corrections to send the monster back to the depths of self control where it hides for months at a time.

I can report as this book goes to the publisher, the Deckers live peacefully with their adopted friend Basher whom I see almost every day. It just so happened when the Deckers were wrapping up Basher's instruction I had a handler's position open, Josh had the interest, and now he's well on his way to becoming a top notch professional trainer.

Conclusion

The vast majority of dog owners I meet seem to fall into two categories: those potentially good handlers who are stifled by fears of crushing their pet's spirit through the exercising of discipline, or those potentially good handlers who are fettered by fears of losing alpha status through relaxed handling. Both categories of good owners would benefit greatly by letting go of their worries before any active handling begins. Our relationship with Canis familiaris is age old and as natural as a person's interactions with extended family. I have found the greatest percentage of our familial dogs possess spirits that are as tough as steel. As a whole, these same tough spirited companions are generally sensitive to leader deference much like children. By relating to your dog in a positive, yet determined, manner there'll be little chance of crushing spirits, or losing your leadership status.

Competitive, defensive, greedy, territorial, controlling, independent, hungry, excitable, engaging, curious, protective, familial, combative, grouchy, affectionate, devoted, courageous, determined, adaptive, resilient, alert, playful, sulking, discerning, bias, yielding and complacent: this long list of adjectives can equally be describing either Homo sapiens, or Canis familiaris. Maybe that's why we get along so well. There is not much imagination required on either part to understand the other. The ability to anthropomorphize is an invaluable tool in dog training. However, getting carried away with empathy or humanizing can be crippling. As your dog's trainer, utilize the anthropomorphizing tool but use it carefully.

My training advice to family and friends as well as clients is always framed within four simple, but monumental concepts.

1. **Appreciate as well as never deny the "animal" in your dog.**
2. **The best handlers are consistent, focused, pleasant and firm (C.F.P.F.).**

3. A trainer's task and limitations lie within shaping the dog's behavior not in changing his personality.
4. You can be a very effective handler even though you may be far from adept.

For those of us who live with an assertive or aggressive canine, it's good to keep in mind there's probably nothing wrong with our companion. He simply came into this world with more available drive and energy than the average dog. It's our job as primary handlers to help him channel and control this extra potential so he can integrate smoothly into human society. The responsibility of keeping innocent parties free from harm due to a dog's hostile behavior falls solely on the shoulders of the primary handlers. **Remember that even good excuses don't help alleviate the pain of a dog bite.**

Baron, Mister and Hector are a few of the dogs I've lived with. They were all my personal family dogs at one time or another. Some did police work, some were competition companions, and others were demonstration dogs. All of them were probably more aggressive than the dog you own, and compared to the thousands of dogs I've handled, I consider them some of the best among canines. By harnessing their energy and helping them direct their drive, all of my aggressive companions were able to safely experience life to its fullest. They were all house dogs and naturally interacted with my wife and children; they lived with me much like your dog lives with you. Taken as a whole they had the potential to display all eight faces of hostility that this book addresses. Yet not a single innocent person was injured by any of them. **The reasons for this safety record lie in these pages and I can sum up those reasons in one word, rules!** Rules for handling, confinement, environmental controls, and rules for interacting with non-handlers are all created and enforced in the name of safety. The rules for managing an aggressive dog are not really difficult to understand or setup; the real challenge lies in their maintenance.

Balance the training relationship with your dog by using earnest deterrents and sincere praise. All dogs can determine within a single moment whether or not a handler is genuine. If you're authentic, a dog will be inclined to follow. If you're not, he'll be inclined to lead. I wish you the best. Now, go do some good!

Made in the USA
Lexington, KY
15 April 2015